To the women whose blood, sweat, and tears paved the way for me to have courage, perseverance, and hope! To them, I will be forever grateful!

Gloria Beatrice Long Overton Harrell—my mother

Mary McCloud Long—my maternal grandmother

Glennie Roundtree Overton—my paternal grandmother

Mary Mann McCloud, Katie Overton, and Ella Perry—my great-grandmothers

ENDORSEMENTS FOR HIDDEN IN PLAIN SIGHT

Kaleema Ameen has bravely stepped forward to describe her own (and others') experiences with men who not only abuse, manipulate and abandon their wives and children, but also bring dishonor on the institution of marriage in their faith communities. Exposing this all-too-common behavior helps women see the 'red flags,' and escape the devastation before it starts, and also provides tools to heal if women have been the victim of abuse and abandonment already.

Suzy Brown, *founder of Midlife Divorce Recovery*
www.midlifedivorcerecovery.com

As a faith and community leader, I believe that Kaleema has gifted all those who are in pastoral care a great resource…I hope that readers use this as a resource to better protect family and friends.

Imam Mika'il Stewart Saadiq,
Chairman of the Imams Council of Michigan
Author of *Islamic Lifestyles in Urban America*

In her book, *Hidden in Plain Sight* Kaleema Overton Ameen has provided information for women from very diverse backgrounds. She has provided 20/20 foresight and 20/20 hindsight. In this book women who are planning to be married will find warning signs to look for before they say I do (20/20 Foresight). Women that have said I do but but were left to hold the covenant of marriage alone will find information to work through the process of understanding what happened to them so they can seek healing for themselves and their families (20/20 Hindsight). No matter where you are on this spectrum you will find nuggets of insight. – *Ronnie L. Riddick, Th.D.,*

Word of Reconciliation Church,
Author of *Words of Grace*
Founder and President of The Transformational Bible Institute

----

Admittedly, when I was asked to review a book centered around relationships, I was somewhat apprehensive. I thought to myself, 'Surely, she could find a better candidate'. I am certainly not a relationship expert, but out of respect and honor for my Muslim sister Kaleema, I decided to delve into it. In the age of political correctness, the Me Too Movement and patriarchy, being a Black Man can be unpopular, so I expected another, 'How to Hate a Black Man book'. I was relieved to be wrong. Hidden in Plain Sight is a survival guide that speaks to the truths and experiences of Women brave enough to not only share their pain and perspectives but also their thoughts and solutions for safe, wholesome committed relationships. This literary art forced me to examine and reevaluate my own thinking and actions. Definitely a must read. I look forward to purchasing copies not only for my daughters and nieces, but for the Brothers in my circle as well. Add it to your library!"-

Kalonji Jama Changa,
Author of *How to Build a Peoples' Army* and
Co-Producer of the film *Organizing Is The New Cool*

Hidden in Plain Sight

Are You Being Groomed for Love-Bombing,
Spirit-Breaking and Abandonment?

Kaleema Overton Ameen

Fulton Books
Meadville, PA

Published by Fulton Books 2023

ISBN 979-8-88731-494-5 (paperback)
ISBN 979-8-88982-235-6 (hardcover)
ISBN 979-8-88731-495-2 (digital)

Printed in the United States of America

CONTENTS

Useful Documents

FOREWORD

On a sunny Saturday afternoon, I was on one of my "check-in" calls with Kaleema. As we were catching up, over the speaker, I exchanged greetings with her family. I could also hear in the background the whooshing of cars down the highway as they traveled to their wedding anniversary resort destination. Looking back, I am sure Kaleema was just as committed to that vacation as she was to her marriage. Nowadays, I am absolutely convinced that she is even more committed to protecting other women and families from what she suffered during that fateful trip.

Kaleema and I became acquainted through our work in the community. She, along with her twin sister and brother-in-law, took the lead to organize a first-of-its-kind conference in Virginia Beach, Virginia. I was honored to be invited as a keynote speaker. From my first encounter with the twins, the kids, and her brother-in-law (a fellow Imam/Minister), I felt so much love and light. I was introduced to all the great projects that they were working on in the Muslim community, interfaith efforts, and the business sector. As the years went by, our families had even spent time together, and we cheered on and supported the milestones reached by each other's children. I guess, in a sense, I have been impressed by the authenticity of Kaleema and her family. We have come to a point in American popular culture where artificiality has almost become an inviolable standard in everything—from food, beauty, personality, and relationships. In the

Holy Quran, Allah (God) says, "O, you who have believed! Be conscious of Allah and say what is straightforward and right. He will then make your deeds righteous and forgive your sins, and whoever obeys Allah, and His Messenger has already achieved a great achievement" (Quran 33 Al-Ahzab, 70–71). Appropriately, these are some of the verses of the Holy Quran that Prophet Muhammad would recite during wedding ceremonies. The verses are a reminder that the foundation of any successful relationship (especially marriage) is authenticity. The Islamic way of life consists of two halves—consciousness of Allah and marriage. It is important to mention that married life is synonymous to family in Islam, because in our tradition, marriage is the prerequisite to family life. The husband and wife create the home, or environment, where they grow together, and their "fruits" (in the form of actions and/or children) will impact the greater biosphere.

This book by our sister Kaleema is a long overdue analysis of habitual abandonment and the sometimes-long-term trauma these behaviors have on women, children, and even other family members. Even though Kaleema centers her Islamic faith throughout the book, the reader will notice careful consideration to deliver an interfaith message for an interfaith crisis. Kaleema does an excellent job of empathizing with the victims and telling their story. She puts well to use analytical skills she has developed in her nearly thirty-year career. I especially appreciate the vulnerable yet composed way in which this book is written and the effort that went into providing a case study for relatability and victim solidarity. As a faith and community leader, I believe that Kaleema has gifted all those who are in pastoral care a great resource. It is my hope that readers are intrigued by the acidulousness within these pages but are also moved to eradicate the abuse of abandonment and use this as a resource to better insulate our friends and families from predation.

Imam Mika'il Stewart Saadiq
President of MANA (Muslim Alliance in North America)
Chairman of the Imams Council of Michigan

My Intentions

After I was made aware that I was a victim of a predatory process, my intention was to use my research on abandonment and narcissism to heal myself. This journey of hope and healing became a labor of love for my sisters as well. In a dark moment, my brother-in-law, Ali, said to me, "*You* have a voice where most women don't! Why *not* you? You can help a lot of women!" I was honored to be a guest columnist in the *Muslim Journal*. Numerous women reached out to me to share their horrific experiences of psychological abuse that went unacknowledged by family, friends, and even the religious community. We will never know the supreme wisdom of Allah (God) when we suffer hardship, but we can trust that His plan is the ultimate plan for our spiritual growth and development. My intention is to be a voice for the voiceless in an effort to heal the deep and often generational wounds of abandonment that leave no physical scars.

ACKNOWLEDGMENTS

I give thanks and acknowledgment to Allah (God), the Creator of all that there is and all that there will ever be for allowing me to write this book to inform, enlighten, and heal! Insha'Allah (God willing)!

SPECIAL THANKS

Special thanks to my family, friends, and community members who supported me through this journey that led up to writing this book. I could never name them all.

I want to especially thank the courageous Imams who supported me and who continue to fight for the rights of all women (Muslim and non-Muslim). This book is *for* the women who have suffered this form of psychological abuse, but please know that there are many men who walk in front of, beside, and behind women who fight to recover and who fight for their rights to be honored.

Imam Ali Abdul Salaam, W. D. Muhammad Islamic Center of Chesapeake, Virginia

Imam Hosea Abdus Salaam, Portsmouth, Virginia

Imam Mika'il Stewart Saadiq, president of MANA (Muslim Alliance of North America) and chairman of the Imams Council of Michigan

Imam Rachid Khould, Crescent Community Center of Virginia Beach, Virginia

Special thanks to Brother Hasan Clay of GLI Counseling Services

INTRODUCTION TO THE BAIT AND SWITCH!

This is a message to women of *all faiths* about the practice of abandonment and the destructive consequences for family and community life. It is a guide, if you will, on how to protect yourself and loved ones by recognizing the red flags in courtship and warning signs that you are being groomed and/or manipulated for abandonment.

This book will provide recommendations on how you can seek justice, heal, and thrive after experiencing this form of emotional, psychological, and economic abuse. It is also a caution to men who are God-conscious and have mothers, daughters, sisters, and nieces whom they want to protect from men who use abandonment as a weapon against their wives or just as a routine practice and way of life.

It is my hope that after reading this book, you will become aware of a distinct type of predator that goes unnoticed while systematically working to groom, deceive, and abuse women and children in full view of—and undetected by—the religious and secular community, family, friends, and colleagues. It is my hope that this book will provide insight to the weaponization of abandonment, the abandonment method of procedure, how narcissism fuels abandonment, the effects on the family and community, the nine red flags in courtship, trauma bonding, how to seek justice and expose the abuse, and finally, steps to recover and thrive after the abuse.

Dr. Jekyll and Mr. Hyde

The step-by-step method of abandonment will be hard to imagine because it is extremely cruel and calculating. Nevertheless, a detailed description of the process is necessary to fully understand this diabolical premeditated form of abuse.

Stage 1—love-bombing. All praise to God! You have found a man who says that he is God-conscious and dedicated to family and community life. You may have met him at your place of worship, at work, or when volunteering in the community. He insists that this is serendipitous and that you are meant to be. He immediately declares his intentions for marriage. He convinces you that *you* are perfect for *him* and that you are perfect for each other. He says that he likes what you like, he wants what you want, and he mirrors everything you say that you aspire to or need out of life. He insists that because you have all these wants, needs, and aspirations in common that you are indeed soul mates. For you, your family, the religious leaders, he has *all* the right answers.

You may even receive a proposal for marriage during the first conversation or an "I love you" very soon in the courtship and too soon to be comfortable as he is extremely persistent. He appears to be practicing the religion and upstanding in the community, and he is gainfully employed. He showers you with compliments, attention, and gifts, and he checks "all the boxes." Even still, your family questions his motives because he is so persistent and so aggressive and just a little too good to be true. He quashes these doubts by lavishing your family and friends and anyone within earshot with his elaborate confessions of his love for you.

He may zero in on the matriarch or patriarch of your family with assurances that he is dedicated to religious and family life and building the community. This leads to a brief courtship, culminating in a quick marriage, as you float to the wedding amid whispers of "too good to be true." You go on to live in relative bliss, give or take. Everyone around you is exclaiming, "You are so blessed! I wish I could find someone like him! Can he help me, my sister, my daughter find a husband?"

Stage 2—demeaning and spirit-breaking. After the "newlywed period," you may start to notice that the compliments and gifts only come when others are watching as they swoon over the two of you. Although the flattery is over the top and usually a huge public display, it never occurs to you that his flattery and attention are not for *your* benefit but for the eyes of those around you. He chooses public displays because you are just a prop on the stage that is his artificial life, and this is the setup for the witnesses to his affection.

All too often, once you are alone again, you find yourself being ignored because you have been placed back on a shelf until his next performance. Over time, you may see hints of jealousy, envy, or unexplained withdrawal from the family. You glimpse odd behavior and demeaning comments that come quick as a flash, then float away on the evening breeze. You forget the sting of the backhanded compliment until the next time…and there it goes again!

You cannot quite put your finger on a strange request, reaction, behavior, or flash of unprovoked anger in his eyes. You get suggestions to do things—or you see him do things—that are out of character or unethical for your way of life. He may even tell you about some heinous immoral or criminal act that he committed and got away with in the past, which can actually be his unknown present. He will do this to gauge your reaction so he can test the limits. He will recount this wicked act of his all while gloating and while you stare in horror, mouth opened in disbelief.

In this stage, you may find that he starts turning his back on you while you are alone or in group settings or even in bed. He may start to voice his displeasure about something in you that he loved before. He will start complaining about something that is not really happening, like your weight loss or weight gain, in an attempt to cause you to be self-conscious. He will do this because if he can get you to demean yourself, there is less work for him to do! He may start to accuse you of trying to sabotage him in some way. For example, if you offer to help him with his business, he will accuse you of trying to take over, disrupt the business, or make him look inferior or incompetent.

At this stage, he will try to turn you against your own family and friends by trying to point out betrayal by them that is not really there. Remember, in stage 1 (love-bombing), he "love-bombed" you *and* your family and friends. Now in stage 2 (demeaning/spirit-breaking), he will say, "Keep them out of our business." He may show irritation at them coming around too much or conveniently separate himself or disappear from family gatherings.

You may find here that his family and/or friends have become distant. That is because he will be running a smear campaign behind your back, planting seeds of deception and lies to cause them to dislike you or to doubt any complaints you may lodge against him. He will wage an all-out premeditated assault on your character unbeknownst to you while simultaneously keeping you between "love-*b*ombing" and "spirit-breaking."

During this time, it is likely that he is sharing your vulnerable secrets or telling family and friends things you allegedly did to him. These things will be easy for him to describe in detail, because in all likelihood, they are the very things that he is doing to you. To further alienate you from family and friends, he may also tell *you* things about *them* to cause you to be distant, such as they are having some sort of family issue from which you should stay clear or that a family member is engaging in some sort of activity, like drinking, drugs, or something else just as undesirable. At this stage, you may encounter anger, bullying, aggression, and in extreme cases, physical abuse.

This stage can go on for months or many, many years depending on how tolerable or unaware you may be of his actions. He can also use your preoccupation with work, children, caring for elderly parents, or even caring for him to work deception while you are not looking.

If he grows tired of all the work it requires to carry on this level of dishonesty, mentally exhausted of his own charade, can no longer abstain from or hide his mental or physical addictions, senses that you have begun to see behind the mask of deception that he is wearing, or he is already love-bombing another victim, then the Broadway-caliber performance is over! At this point, he will begin to set up for stage 3—abandonment and discard.

Stage 3—abandonment/discard. This is the final stage and will be the quickest step and most painful assault on your humanity. He will start to uncharacteristically explode, or if the physical aggression and/or abuse began in stage 2 (demeaning and spirit-breaking), it will likely escalate at this point.

He may also display or have symptoms of some sort of addictive behavior. That is because narcissists are also prone to having hidden addictions to things such as prescription and/or street drugs, alcohol, sex, pornography, or whatever brings instant mental or physical satisfaction. However, while engaging in these hidden addictions, he is likely to continue to function professionally and socially.

If you are fortunate enough to recognize this stage—and unfortunate to still be around after stage 1 (love-bombing)—then this is the time to pay close attention and protect yourself! He may start to disappear from the home for hours or days, even weeks, to indulge in one of his hidden addictions or some secret life he is building. He will then return to start love-bombing you all over again.

Finally, after much ado, he disappears for good. He exits stage left from his performance as the curtain closes behind him. His *performance* as the husband—such as it was—is over. You stand emotionally bludgeoned, dazed, and confused as he uncaringly moves on to the next target without a glance back because this, my sister, is a method of procedure. You were not his first victim and will not be his last. In fact, in all likelihood, he was already grooming the next victim who was in stage 1 (love-bombing) and he was building his new life while you were in stage 2 (demeaning/spirit-breaking), which is the reason for his clean abrupt break. Now you stand here traumatized in stage 3 (abandonment and discard).

Frozen in the aftermath, you look around and see the children, family, friends, and community members lying scattered in the carnage. They are all collateral damage, victims of a war no one knew he was waging…well, except him, because this was a premeditated act. It is at this point that all those things in the back of your mind come rushing forward as you connect odd behavior, unexplained absences, uncharacteristic outbursts, mood swings, and being engaged with the family to being suddenly withdrawn.

This savage discard may be a disappearing act while you are out of the home because he doesn't have the guts to face you, or it can be part of a full-fledged verbal or physical assault, all of which he will blame on you because he has already set the stage. This discard is perhaps the first and only time that you will see the true person in all his hate, rage, and absence of God-consciousness. This is the first and last glimpse of the person who lives behind the mask that he has on constant display. That is because up to this point, you have been dealing with the "publicity agent." Unfortunately, it is far too late to protect yourself because the bullet has left the chamber. The marriage or commitment you thought you shared was nothing more than a manufactured smoke screen for his hidden life.

You have been (1) love-bombed, (2) demeaned, and (3) abandoned all in that order. In all honesty, this is one of only two possible outcomes when dealing with the narcissist: option 1, abandonment, *or* option 2, a long-term marriage filled with lies, deception, psychological abuse, and/or a second hidden—or open— life outside of the marriage. The process he will use is identical each time, but the length of each stage can vary. *This is the end of life as you knew it and of stage 3—abandonment and discard.* Breathe…if you can.

Forget about him being remorseful and apologetic or asking for forgiveness because he believes that he is entitled to do this. In addition, this is the method of procedure that he is accustomed to executing. Check his track record, and you will find a history of abandonment and disappearing acts from family and/or the religious community, as well as betrayal. Yes, betrayal! Abandonment is premeditated and an ongoing betrayal in three stages: before, during, and after the commission of the abuse. The abuse inflicted may be on four levels: spiritual, emotional, physical, and economic. Therefore, the healing likewise will have to reach all levels to be fully effective. Astonishingly, his overwhelming sense of entitlement protects him from any guilt or remorse. In his world, there is no one worthy of his apology—and since the love-bombing is over—my dear sister, which *now* includes *you!*

But let us face the facts. You have been catfished! Not online but *live*, up close, and in person! In plain view of family, friends, your religious community, and colleagues. They, too, have been catfished! They may be completely unaware because the narcissist is a professional at compartmentalizing his life. Family, friends, community members, and colleagues will be kept in neat silos. He will rarely allow interaction, and if he does, he will be in full control of the depth, length, and type of interaction so he can continue to operate his deception undetected. This is how he will hide in plain sight!

CHAPTER 1

"Ain't I a Woman?"[1]

To be clear, I am not a psychologist, therapist, or marriage counselor. Writing this book was unexpectedly one of the many organic steps of my healing from the trauma of narcissistic manipulation, psychological abuse, and abandonment. This book came about because I am a policy analyst. I have built a successful career analyzing policies, procedures, and processes for almost thirty years. I decided to analyze the process of abandonment for my own understanding, healing, and restoration. I was also informed by a fellow survivor that it was an orchestrated process that she also endured. I approached analyzing abandonment with the same methodology that I use professionally as a policy analyst because researching a process is a place of ease and familiarity for me.

The role of a policy analyst is to study the impact that a policy or procedure has on organizations, individuals, or social groups. A policy analyst also studies political, educational, or social trends,

---

[1] "Ain't I a Woman?" is the term coined by Sojourner Truth (1797–1883) during her speech "Ain't I a Woman?" delivered in 1851 at the Women's Rights Convention, Old Stone Church in Akron, Ohio.

ideas, and strategies. They do this to develop observations and provide reports on findings in an attempt to influence laws and/ or policies. The goal of the policy analyst is to research potential impacts so they can make expert recommendations for improvement. For example, a policy analyst may research and make recommendations on a policy or program designed to provide counseling, job opportunities, and shelter to abused women. The analyst will strengthen the program by identifying gaps in the process, developing corrective action plans, and/or giving an expert opinion that changes or informs legislation and funding levels.

That is what I have attempted to do with this book, to research the practice and/or procedure of abandonment and to study the impact on women, children, and the community. In addition, I hope to provide information, recommendations, and steps—which include recognizing the red flags—that will positively influence how we protect the most vulnerable populations in our communities.

In some ways, this book may be premature because I am still healing. In addition, admittedly, I am not among the most vulnerable in the population. However, this book was necessary *now* because others could possibly suffer this abuse if I wait on my own healing. This is about the countless voiceless women who have endured this form of psychological, emotional, spiritual, and economic abuse. You will hear my story but also the stories of the women interviewed for this book. I ask you to please bear with me as I walk you through the step-by-step procedure for this type of deception that is often the result of narcissistic manipulation, abuse, and/or abandonment. Dr. Martin Luther King Jr. quoted the Bible when he said, "To whom much is given, much is required." Therefore, it is incumbent upon me to use this book and all resources available to me to educate and support those who will suffer the greatest harm under this egregious and oppressive practice. Those who will suffer the greatest harm and are most vulnerable are women who, because of abandonment, will be unable to provide food, clothing, and shelter for themselves, their children, or elderly parents under their care.

While analyzing the effects of abandonment, I thought it was important to include accounts of several courageous and compassionate women. These women are from different racial/ethnic, religious, educational, and/or socioeconomic backgrounds. To compile the case studies, I identified several cases of abandonment through referrals and from professionals in the field treating clients recovering from the trauma of abandonment. Some of the interviewees had completed counseling; others are still under care. All the interviewees volunteered for this book and wanted to do so anonymously because they are still in various stages of recovery and do not want to be subjected to additional abuse and/or scrutiny.

To start this project, I reviewed many sources, including but not limited to literature, medical journals and periodicals, media, videos, federal health and social service websites, and support group blogs for women in transition from divorce, abuse, and/or abandonment. I did this to establish a basic understanding of the phenomenon of abandonment. I even came across at least one conversation in a blog where men were instructing others on how to successfully commit this abuse without legal ramifications by avoiding marriage licenses and/or marriage contracts. I studied the literature on abandonment, which led me to the connection to narcissism. I used this information to develop interview questions. The full interviews are in the appendices. The questions were divided into three categories/stages: (1) love-bombing, (2) spirit-breaking, and (3) abandonment/discard. In addition, each participant was asked to give insight to things they wished they had done to protect themselves or questions they wished they had asked to better assess the danger. Finally, they were asked to provide final thoughts and advise on how to move forward and thrive after the abuse.

The method of interviews included having participants respond to questions in writing or by recording their responses. This was followed up by Zoom and/or telephone interviews. I was one of the case studies; therefore, I engaged an accomplished writer/editor to conduct and compile my interview so there was no conflict of interest. Thus, I became Case Study No. 5. Using a multiple-case study approach allowed for a more in-depth understanding of narcissistic manipulation, abuse, and abandonment as a whole. Through comparison of similarities and differences of the individual cases, I began to recognize a pattern. You will also see the pattern and the evidence of the very uncanny similarities of the husbands, partners, or fiancés. Case similarities included but were not limited to the ladies' responses to the questions about themselves and their partners, the process or steps that led to their abuse, the timing of events, psychological effects on the victims, and the recovery processes.

I included the experiences of these women because this problem is not a "poor people's" problem or a "Muslim" problem or a "black people's" problem or a "white privilege" problem. This is not even a young peoples' problem. This problem exists in all communities and slips under the radar because some people feel comfortable turning a blind eye when the abuse is not in their backyard. They can easily ignore the abuse if there are no visible scars, black eyes, busted lips, or broken bones to offend the onlooker. In addition, some women may also believe they are "safe" from this predatory behavior because of their religion, education, or economic status. However, abuse from narcissistic manipulation and abandonment is very likely to be committed by some of the most accomplished leaders in our communities as they hide behind their status and say, "You know me"—meaning their accomplishments—"so don't believe what your own eyes and ears are showing and telling you. Believe what *I am* telling you instead because I am…[insert any title, degree, charitable act, or socioeconomic status]."

These diverse women bravely shared their experiences with me about the narcissistic manipulation and/or abuse and abandonment to which they were subjected. They provided very personal accounts of entering what they thought was a safe place in a marriage or engagement only to be subjected to constant narcissistic manipulation, betrayal, and deception, ending with the horror of a planned, orchestrated, and premeditated abandonment or unplanned divorce. They went on to provide advice on how you could recover after living through this form of psychological cruelty. Make no mistake. Psychological abuse is one of the *most* common forms of domestic violence that leaves no physical evidence, so it is a "perfect crime."

These survivors offer true words of wisdom, love, and selflessness for your protection, healing, and success! I applaud these women for daring to be heard and to allow their love for themselves, each other, and *you* to inspire them to tell their stories.

The women in the case studies range in age from midthirties to midfifties. They are Muslims and Christians, African American, South American, Caribbean, and Caucasian. They are women whose line of work include but is not limited to education, retired military, behavioral therapist, and social media influencers, just to name a few. But as different as they are in their demographics and accomplishments, one of the things they all have in common is the psychological trauma of abandonment. You will see references to their case studies peppered throughout the book; however, a full detailed account of each woman's experience can be found in the appendices.

In this book, I speak primarily from the voice of a Muslim because I am a Muslim. But I am also a mother, an African American, a sister, a daughter, a niece, an accomplished professional (considered an expert in my field), an avid volunteer, and a productive member of society. I wear many hats, and I have many sisters. The women in this book are my sisters although some are not Muslim and some are not African American. We are sisters in our experiences and sisters in our determination to reclaim our spirit after emerging through what is sure to be one of the most pivotal events in our lives. Some of us are healed; some of us are still healing, but all of us can offer guardrails, litmus tests, and red flag warnings to avoid the trauma that we—and our families—have suffered at the hands of narcissistic manipulation, abuse, and/or abandonment. When abandonment is used as a punishment or weapon, it is indeed psychological and economic abuse. My sisterhood with these ladies, albeit from the horrific circumstances of "the ugly evil" of abandonment, runs true and deep. We are bonded by our accounts of betrayal and psychological trauma…*but* we are also bonded by our recovery, hope, resilience, and triumph!

During our lives as adults—or even some children—there will be various points in our journey where our lives are split asunder. Lives can be torn into pieces upon the death of a spouse, parent, child, or by some life-threatening illness, tragic accident, or near-death experience. From that point on, we start to speak of our lives in terms of "before and after" that event because that experience has created a vast canyon in our lives. We have emerged from an abyss; we have survived, and now we are entering an uncertain world, seeing and navigating it through new eyes and with new fears.

Abandonment by a spouse or significant other will also split your life into "before and after," especially upon the realization that this was inflicted intentionally, was part of a psychosis, and you were a pawn in this repulsive practice. It will split your life into *before* you were aware of this ugly evil and *after* you were aware of this ugly evil. The realization that there is a whole subset of the community who uses this as a way of life just because they can or to punish their wives is horrific. The idea that these people have done this before and will do this again is also horrific. The realization that your life with this person was a lie and every memory that the two of you built was a means to an orchestrated end is, again, horrific. There is an African proverb that says, "The tree remembers what the ax forgets." The abandoning narcissist is indeed an ax that will systematically chop away at your spirit and then conveniently forget the abuse and gaslight all those around you in an effort to rewrite history.

Let me say it again: psychological abuse *is* domestic violence! My examination and analysis of this process revealed that this phenomenon of abandonment is indeed psychological abuse resulting in trauma that affects all communities, religions, socioeconomic groups, and ages. A common denominator abandonment has with physical and sexual abuse is that, in most cases, it still goes largely unreported. To compound this problem, abandonment of a spouse—unless they are disabled and/or in need of short- or long-term medical care—in most states is *not* a crime. But not being a crime is light-years away from being harmless or ethical. This method of weaponizing abandonment is wholly uncivilized and a violation of marital commitments, family ties, and human decency regardless of religion. Nevertheless, abandonment has yet to be fully addressed in the courts, although they do address desertion, which is a different issue that will be explained later.

You may be asking yourself, "If abandonment is not a crime, then why does it matter?" I implore you to think about how long women had been physically and sexually abused in this country before it was recognized as a crime. It was not until the 1980s that physical violence against women and/or your wife was taken seriously enough that a bill was passed on this issue. Even then, law enforcement and the legal system often turned a blind eye to physical or sexual abuse by a spouse. If it took that long (almost two hundred years) in the history of this country for violence that left physical scars to be addressed, how long do you think it will take for psychological abuse and violence to be fully acknowledged and adequately addressed in a court of law?

There was little or no focus on violence against women until the late 1980s and early 1990s. The Violence Against Women Act was passed in 1994.[2] This was the first federal legislation acknowledging that domestic violence and sexual assault against women is a crime, 218 years after the US declared its independence! But let's give this whole issue some deeper thought, shall we?

This country was colonized by the British in the late 1500s. It was over two hundred years before the first bill of rights was enacted and then almost another two hundred years before this country passed a bill on violence against women. In 1993, the World Conference on Human Rights and the Declaration on the Elimination of Violence Against Women both announced that domestic violence against women was a public health policy concern and a human rights issue.

Clearly, the state of affairs for women in this country has greatly improved. We even have a female vice president of the United States, but women and girls still remain at high risk mentally, physically, and financially. According to the Centers for Disease Control's National Intimate Partner and Sexual Violence Survey, nearly 1 in 4 women have experienced contact sexual violence, physical violence, and/or stalking by an intimate partner during their lifetime and reported

---

[2] VAWA was written by then senator Joseph R. Biden and signed into law by President Bill Clinton, Title IV of the Violent Crime Control and Law Enforcement Act, H. R. 3355.

also some form of intimate partner violence. In addition, 43 million women have experienced psychological aggression by an intimate partner in their lifetime. Tragically, on average, 70 women are shot or killed by an intimate partner *each month*!

The WHO (World Health Organization) reports that 1 in 3 women worldwide experience violence in their lifetime. "Violence against women is *endemic* in every country and culture, causing harm to millions of women and their families and has been exacerbated by the COVID-19 pandemic," according to the WHO director general.[3] His statement speaks volumes with the use of the word *endemic*, which is a disease that is stable, ongoing, and predictable, as opposed to an *epidemic*, which is sudden and unpredictable. Can you imagine the awareness we can create if (1) we continue to use predictability of abuse (such as red flags) to teach women how to recognize the signs and thus protect themselves and (2) if more women can feel empowered to report psychological abuse and cruelty from abandonment so they can be documented and added to the statistics of this endemic of domestic violence? Do you wonder how over 250,000 women and girls went missing in the United States in 2021 (194,673 under twenty-one and 62,552 over twenty-one) and it has not been on the breaking news every day? Do you wonder how women are killed in their homes, on dates, randomly in the streets, victims of trafficking or go away on vacations and never come back? Globally, a girl or woman is killed every eleven minutes by someone they know and/or their intimate partner.

I ask you, Are we going to endure another two-hundred-year cycle before abandonment is recognized as a crime? I ask you, *Ain't I a woman* whose mental and psychological health and well-being are worthy of protection from clear and present danger? *Ain't I a woman* to be protected from intentional, premeditated, and orchestrated assault on my psyche? *Ain't I a woman* with inalienable, absolute, and incontrovertible rights? I submit to you that *we are*—by rite of the Holy Quran, the Holy Bible, the Torah, and the Constitution of the

---

[3] Press release: "Devastatingly pervasive: 1 in 3 women globally experience violence. *Younger women among those most at risk: WHO*" (March 9, 2021).

United States—owed justice and equality and a life free from assault on our dignity, our spirit, our bodies, and our very humanity! Ain't I a woman? Do we get a hashtag? #WomensPsychologicalHealthMatters!

CHAPTER 2

The Secret Art of Weaponizing Abandonment

Important note: Throughout this book, I will often use Allah when referring to God because I am a Muslim. I want to be clear that Allah *is the Arabic word used by Muslims to indicate the one true God and is the same God referenced by Jews as Yahweh and by Christians as God. Some Christians in Arab-speaking countries also use* Allah *to reference God. Hopefully, I successfully respect both Christianity and Islam in my biblical and Quranic references and show the similarities in the belief systems on this particular topic.*

Abandonment should not be confused with a planned separation or divorce, which is within the rights of every individual. Nor should it be seen just as being left on the side of the road or in a desolate place. By law, *abandonment* is defined as leaving and/or removing support from the marriage, family, or home without warning or notice. This does not include separation by mutual consent. Simply put, abandonment is just walking off from the home, family, or marriage. This includes disappearing from—or the new term, *ghosting*—the wife or family without warning and no further contact or explanation. This behavior is most commonly found in narcissists, and narcissism is more commonly diagnosed in men than women. In a new study on narcissism, it was revealed that men, on average, are more narcissistic than women. In addition, "the study compiled 31 years of narcissism research and found that men consistently scored higher in narcissism across multiple generations and regardless of age.[4] Narcissism is associated with various interpersonal dysfunctions, including an inability to maintain healthy long-term relationships, unethical behavior, and aggression."

Abandonment is a form of emotional and psychological abuse that often goes unacknowledged because there "appears" to be no physical damage. Sadly, much like physical and sexual abuse, due to the lack of understanding of this form of psychological cruelty, the victim is often blamed for their own abuse and/or shamed into staying silent. Although this form of psychological abuse has become an increasing problem in the Muslim community, abandonment can be found in any community regardless of religion, race, ethnicity, education, or socioeconomic status.

Communities of faith are fighting against this practice through ongoing education and implementing the natural religious safeguards when it comes to courtship and marriage. Nevertheless, men with less-than-honorable intent use deceptive tactics to get around these safeguards. Consequently, far too many women are reporting abandonment that leads to spiritual, emotional, and financial distress of women, children, and the religious community.

Oh believers treat women with kindness for
if you dislike them; it is quite possible that you

---

[4] University at Buffalo, "Men Tend to Be More Narcissistic than Women, Study Finds," ScienceDaily (March 4, 2015), www.sciencedaily.com/releases/2015/03/150304104040.htm.

dislike something which Allah makes a source of
abundant good. (The Holy Quran 4:19)

Husbands, love your wives, as Christ loved
the church and gave of himself for her... (The
Holy Bible, Ephesians 5:25)

For communities of faith, family life is the heart of the community. If the practice of abandonment is not exposed and extinguished, we cannot aspire to create strong families and build a thriving community. We should create communities where *all* members are free and safe from mental or physical abuse. Unfortunately, abuse in any form has the potential to change the trajectory of an entire family or community, and abuse from abandonment is no exception.

While it is not the norm and is in no way sanctioned by any religion, abandonment is still a growing disease in religious communities across the country that must be eradicated. Women in religious communities are especially vulnerable to acts of abandonment because of the often-short courtship period practiced in religious communities. Unfortunately, men with a hidden agenda can twist the short courtship, which is meant to be a protection, to their advantage. Therefore, it is important that women approached for marriage, and those who care about them, give extra scrutiny to any potential spouse.

Abandonment is an act of oppression and psychological violence. *Make no mistake about it. Abandonment is more often than not a process and routine that is practiced by men with ill-intent.* In addition, there is a clear modus operandi that is conducted by men who perform this heinous act. This book will expose the method of abandonment, which includes but may not be limited to (1) love-bombing, (2) demeaning and spirit-breaking, and (3) discard/abandonment, the final step in the process.

Allah indeed has heard the plea of the
woman who pleads with Thee about her husband
and complains to Allah; and Allah hears the con-

tentions of both of you. Surely Allah is Hearing, Seeing. (The Holy Quran 58:1)

Likewise, husbands, live with your wives in an understanding way, showing honor to the woman as the weaker vessel, since they are heirs with you of the grace of life, so that your prayers may not be hindered. (The Holy Bible, 1 Peter 3:7)

CHAPTER 3

Exposing the Abandonment Method of Procedure

Recognizing the red flags as well as this cookie-cutter process is the first step to protecting yourself or family members from manipulation, abandonment, and/or abuse. The scenario described in the introduction is a result of psychological and/or narcissistic manipulation, abuse, and abandonment.

You may be asking yourself, "How does narcissism relate to the abandonment of families?" According to experts in the field, such as Dr. Rhonda Freeman, Dr. Linda Martinez-Lewi, Dr. Jean Collins, Lynn Nichols, and others who are cited in this book, people with narcissistic personality disorder exploit personal relationships to elevate their self-image or to have their physical or emotional needs met. Their own family members are not off-limits to this exploitation. Emotionally, a narcissist is often like a child in an adult's body. Their emotional intelligence was very likely stunted as a child usually because of some sort of childhood abuse, dysfunction, overindulgence, or quite possibly the same abandonment he inflicts upon others.

"In a way, this regression makes sense. Narcissistic personality disorder or a narcissistic style often develops due to early trauma or family influences that can leave aspects of a person stuck at an emotionally young age."[5] "A lack of empathy is often considered to be one of the distinctive features of narcissism. However, this is not entirely the case. The criteria for the formal psychiatric diagnosis of narcissistic personality disorder includes 'lacks empathy,' but this characteristic has an important qualifier, not just that he *lacks* empathy but that he is *unwilling* to recognize or identify with the feelings and needs of others."[6] The covert or white-knight narcissist will elaborately fake this quality during the love-bombing stage.

According to *Psychology Today*, a person with narcissistic tendencies may fake vulnerability by opening up about past hardships. Yet three factors may be flags that this is manipulation versus vulnerability. First, the person uses a personal hardship to cause *you* to feel guilty. Second, he excuses himself from accountability for present acts by utilizing a trauma from the past. Third, the person redirects attention to himself by broadcasting a personal struggle, which takes him back to no accountability for his actions. "These tactics allow a narcissistic individual the opportunity to play the victim in order to control and dominate others."[7]

Case Study No. 4. "Not only was he manipulative toward my daughter and me but he was also very manipulative toward his parents as well. His relationship with them was severely damaged. While we were still married, his parents had moved out of state to get away from his verbal and emotional abuse. When they found out we were divorcing, they moved back to help him coparent our daughter. Eventually, his parents had enough of his manipulation and abusive treatment, so they disowned him. They reached out to me so they

---

5 Dan Neuharth, "12 Ways Narcissist Behave like Children."
6 Mary C. Lamia, "Do Narcissist Actually Lack Empathy?" (2020).
7 Erin Leonard, "Why a Narcissist May Seem Emotionally Intelligent" (2021).

could have a relationship with their granddaughter. We—the grandparents and I—have built a healthy friendship, and he has no further connection with his parents."

Case Study No. 5. "When I complained to my new husband that his way of talking to me was condescending and bully-like, he gave me three days of the silent treatment. This was our first Ramadan together. When I approached him to discuss the issue, because I don't have time for silent treatments, he seemed like he was hurt that I would say this about him. Then he said that this [condescending/aggressive way of talking] was how he was used to dealing with his previous wives. I was his fourth wife. I was shocked that he was admitting this but thought that it was a sign of sincerity in trying to mend his ways. He behaved like a child being chastised but did not really apologize, just said he would correct the behavior. He didn't, of course."

According to experts in the field, everything narcissists do is for the purpose of getting control, attention; admiration, protecting their ego and/or deflecting shame from themselves onto whoever is closest to them, usually the spouse and/or children. It is easier to break this down into steps of the process because they are small pebbles thrown over time that build a mountain of psychological control and abuse. Let's take a closer look at the process.

Stage 1—Love-Bombing

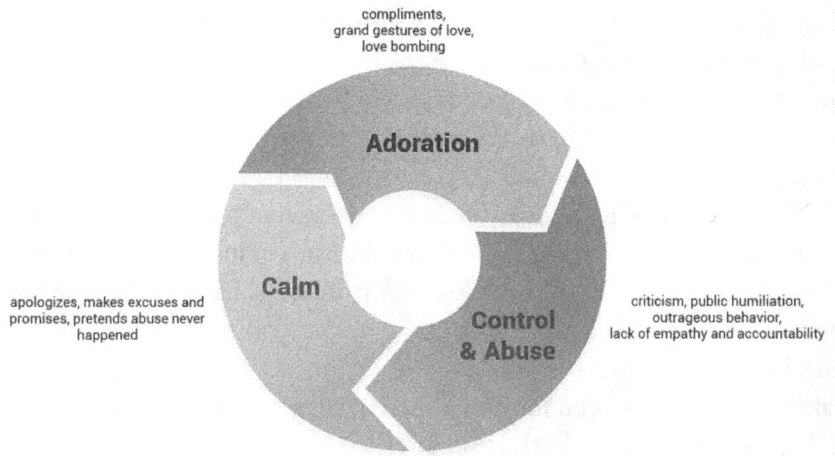

Love-bombing occurs at the beginning of the courtship. He will shower you with over-the-top attention, compliments, and promises. He will show interest and charm in the initial stages. Unfortunately, for most narcissists, courtship and marriage are simply a means to an end, which is to get positive attention and physical satisfaction to boost his ego and self-esteem. He will be relentless in his declarations of love and compliments and gifts. However, his main goal is never out of focus for him, which is to obtain self-gratification through this partnership.

Case Study No. 1. "During our second conversation, he referred to me as beloved and said that he was my future intended husband. I was a bit concerned about him calling me beloved so quickly. He did not know me well enough to be using terms of endearment so early. It's as though he was forcing me further into a relationship we weren't even in yet."

Case Study No. 2. "Early on, he often told me I was his soul mate and was very eager to spend time with my family. He even called my uncle and asked him if he could marry me."

Case Study No. 3. "He insisted he was ready for marriage or commitment immediately. He went into that right away. He started sending pictures of houses for us to consider and wedding venues from day 2 or day 3. He made sure he was in contact with me every day, all day. There was an excessive amount of phone calls, face time, and text messages. Not an hour went by without there being contact between us. I just thought that this was someone who was extremely interested in me. But it was very, very excessive. At a certain point, I remember feeling overwhelmed."

Case Study No. 5. "Although we volunteered in the same community, we had no personal contact. However, in our first personal written communication, he asked me if I would be his wife. He said he had been watching me volunteer in the community for a while and knew that I was the perfect wife for him. I was taken aback and said that I had not been looking for marriage at that time. He insisted if I 'take a leap of faith' that he could show me that he would be a good husband for me and support system for my son."

Uncommitted "short-term" physical relationships are forbidden in religious communities. Because of this, he may resort to jumping from marriage to marriage. He will do this to keep up his image as a married Muslim or Christian and have the emotional and physical attention that he needs to fuel his ego. He will attempt to maintain his status and reputation as a family man, using the marriage and/ or religion as a cover. He will hide behind these props (the wife will be a prop as well) to mask his true intent while he works deception or lives an alternate life. Nevertheless, he will soon lose interest as the thrill of the hunt and honeymoon period are over, and he does not want to fulfill the expectations for long-term commitment and companionship. If he feels that he has conquered the challenge of obtaining, manipulating, and/or controlling you or that you detect his deception, he will flee.

Some narcissists can manage a long-term marriage; however, it is likely to be filled with manipulation, abuse, infidelity, and/or a hidden lifestyle away from home. He will be full of contradictions. For example, while he can be quite charming, he will have very few close friends of his own, or although he talks about family life, he will keep you separated from them.

His strategy is to compartmentalize his life, having family, friends, and colleagues in easily manageable silos, because he is always setting up for the final abandonment stage. To do this, he will discourage you from having any real bonds with his family and friends, citing their deficiencies or dysfunction and that he is only trying to protect you from them. This strategy will aid him during the final abandonment process. Remember, he is manipulating his family and friends as well to prevent them from coming to your aid even if they have sympathy for you as a human being. He will also create ways to separate you from your own family and friends by saying they are not trustworthy, accuse them of some infraction, or accuse you of being disloyal to him by maintaining these friendships.

Case Study No. 2. "He always seemed to be very well rehearsed when we were around family and friends. But he was a different person to me than the one he presented to his family, friends, and colleagues."

Case Study No. 4. "Another warning came when my friend from college invited me to visit her in Santa Fe. By this time, my ex and I had been dating for a few months He made a big deal about me going to Santa Fe alone. He accused me of finding someone else when I went down there."

Case Study No. 5. "I never met any of his friends. Although I often had friends that would visit our home, he never once invited a friend to our home or to any family or social events that we attended together. In hindsight, I realize that he never introduced me to any of his friends to establish relationships even after four years of marriage."

Stage 2—Demeaning and Spirit-Breaking

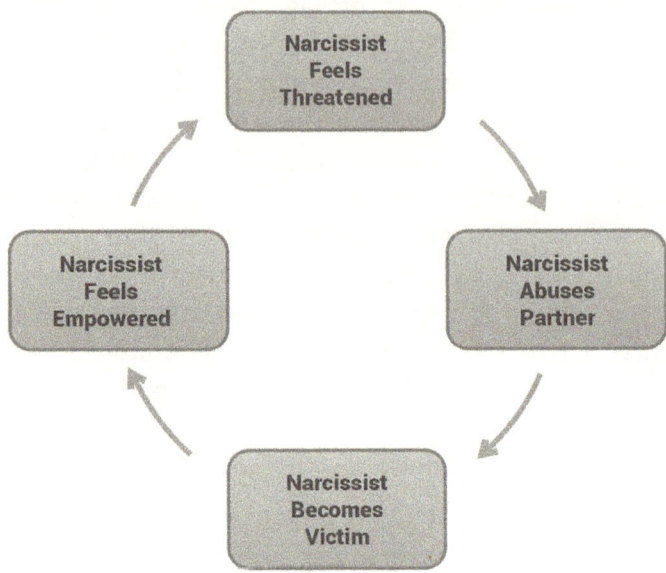

Dr. Rhonda Freeman is a clinical neuropsychologist who works with patients diagnosed with neurological conditions and writes for *Psychology Today*. She explained that "psychopaths are prone to interact through manipulation and to use others for their sole benefit, even if this creates pain and devastation for the target. Extending love and care to them will *not* impact the expression of pathology from the psychopathic partner."[8]

The narcissist is a very skilled actor, and sometimes he will mask his anger and displeasure from you and those around you. This is not in an attempt to control his emotions but instead is an attempt to control the narrative. He is always consumed with thoughts of displeasure in you and in himself, and instead of trying to resolve these imagined problems, he will instead plan ways to abandon. You will find that the narcissist always seems distracted, not fully present, or preoccupied. Sometimes this dissatisfaction happens without you even knowing anything has changed due to him being a very skilled

---

[8] Rhonda Freeman, "6 Obstacles to a Relationship with a Psychopath" (2015).

actor and manipulator. While in this stage, there are many ways the narcissist will choose to diminish you and to inflict punishment and pain that will leave no visible scars for the public as these are some of the ways that he will hide in plain sight.

The Silent Treatment

A common tactic is "the silent treatment." This will typically be the response to any small infraction or no infraction at all because he will create a situation for which he will make you the blame and then he will inflict the punishment. For example, you may call him to say you are going to be late coming home from work, so you will have to pick up dinner along the way. He may say, "That is fine. Take your time." But when you arrive at home, he will start an argument about you being late and that he doesn't want takeout. When you remind him of his approval, he will gaslight you (twist the facts) by saying that the argument is your fault for being late and not having time to cook dinner and that you should be a better planner. He will insist that you have ruined the night, then deploy the silent treatment that may last for days on end. This silent treatment may go on until you apologize for working late, not preparing dinner, and/or for the argument that he orchestrated.

The Put-Down

Another go-to is the put-down. Sometimes this put-down will be very subtle, like a compliment that is laced with an insult, and other times, the put-down will come in an unexpected burst of unprovoked anger.

Case Study No. 5. "I turned down a job that had a significant pay cut. It wasn't a big deal because I was just testing the market. He was shockingly very angry, and he said, 'How much money do you need anyway? I would have to work two jobs to get that type of money! What do you do with your money anyway?' Later, when I happily told him that I found a job with acceptable pay, he said, 'I guess you do know your worth.'"

This is a double whammy because the covert narcissist does *not* really want you to be successful. Who are you to be happy and successful? Who are you to dare get what he covets? Why are you so selfish, wanting success for yourself? The spotlight is for him! Of course, there is logically room for both of you to succeed if this were a normal functional relationship. But in the narcissistic world, there is only room for *one* success story, and it is not you!

Sabotage

You must always look out for sabotage. He will take any opportunity to sabotage you during his secret smear campaign that he will undoubtedly wage against you before his exit. This sabotage can be mental, physical, financial, or spiritual. It can come in the form of (1) creating emotional chaos that will prevent you from seeing his deception, (2) short disappearing acts or threats of and/or acts of physical abuse, (3) hiding money or property, or (4) withdrawing from his religious obligations, family, or community and leave you holding the bag.

Case Study No. 2. "Sometimes he tried to make me look bad for his advantage. He told others that I was melodramatic and a drama queen. One of his friends described our relationship like he was a dog on a hill guarding a bone that he does not really want. He said that when some other dog comes around, he will charge down the hill, but as long as no one else wants the bone, then he will just sit on the hill. I was offended by this description."

Case Study No. 5. "He told me that he had to drop his family member off at his sister's school for an event, saying several times that she was making a big deal of it, but it was nothing really. It happened to be on the same day as a family outing we planned at the beach. He said he will be right back, but when I saw that he put on a suit, I said, 'You're pretty dressed up just to drop her off.' He said [with irritation at her request], 'Oh, she wants me to walk her inside. It's nothing important. She is always making a big deal about nothing. I will be right back.' He was gone for several hours. When he returned, we went to a wonderful family day at the beach with my son. A week or so later, I called his family member to invite her to his event. She asked me why I had not attended a very important event for our family member who received a big award! I was taken by surprise and embarrassed. I told her he didn't invite me and I was not aware that it was an award ceremony for her. I was very embarrassed that it seemed to her that I had blown off a very important day for his family member."

As part of sabotage, he will also report to family, friends, colleagues, the neighbor or mailman, or even your children—as they are not off-limits—that you are, in fact, trying to sabotage him, his image, or his success. The smear campaign where he plays the role of the victim will alienate you from his family and sometimes, unknowingly, from your own family and friends.

Another example is, he will start a fight on an important day—like a birthday, anniversary, or family outing—and say you ruined the event by not apologizing for the argument that he created. After it is sufficiently ruined, he will deploy the silent treatment, extract an apology from *you*, then love-bombing, and back to normal behavior. However, he may use this orchestrated argument as his opportunity to abandon. He will constantly rinse and repeat this process in small morsels until he is ready to serve up the entire poisonous meal with the kill shot.

Case Study No. 1. "Whenever I sat with my former intended [fiancée], he was so attentive. We had such great conversations. He seemed to adore me and gave me beautiful compliments. However, after sit-downs, he took a long time to get back to my *wakil* [adviser] about our next session. This caused me a great deal of anxiety. I could not understand how he could be so into me when we were with the wakil, but it would take my wakil reaching out to him, then wait a couple of weeks to respond, and then we would all meet again. He showered me with attention and compliments at the meetings with the wakil but took days/weeks to return messages. This was the routine that kept me in anxiety."

Case Study No. 2. "He constantly canceled or backed out of commitments. It was one disappointment after another. I never felt like I mattered or that my feelings were important. Even though he would ask me what I wanted, he always found reasons why my choice wasn't going to work for him. Then he always reminded me that he was a strong man. He always said that strong men don't let women control them."

Case Study No. 3. "The very moment after the wedding, when we were starting on the honeymoon, he went into full-fledged demeaning mode. He was criticizing me and putting me down. Our honeymoon was actually very traumatic for me. He left me alone at a place because he was mad. He did the most abrupt, abrasive things out of the blue on the honeymoon. His demeaning and breakdown started right after the wedding. From that point on, it was hell. Soon after the honeymoon, he left for several weeks."

Case Study No. 4. "My daughter and I have discovered that we no longer have a preference in certain situations in life after what we experienced. When we are asked something as simple as 'What would you like for dinner?' we have found that we never have an answer. That is because during my marriage, my ex would ask the same questions. If I responded, 'Oh, chipotle sounds good,' he would then reply, 'Oh, I don't want that. I want _____.' It came down to me trying to guess what he wanted instead of me having a prefer- ence. In actuality, he stripped me of a part of who I am. My daughter finds herself doing the same thing, being unable to state her wants."

Case Study No. 5. "I called to say I was unexpectedly with my sister and brother-in-law in the hospital. He insisted I stay and take care of the family and said, 'Send them my prayers.' When I arrived home, he was distant and visibly angry. When I asked about his mood, he yelled that I was gone all day and began to verbally attack me. He continued, now standing over me while I was sitting. When I looked confused about his exaggerated behavior, he said, 'Since you have that stupid look on your face...!' I finally verbally defended myself, which in hindsight allowed him to intensify the argument. Prior to this, we had never argued beyond a difference of opinion, which was mostly something philosophical. He gave me the silent treatment for two days, then anniversary gifts, then the abandonment two days later."

Revealing Your Private Information or Withholding Positive Achievements

The next tactic used to punish you is to reveal your private information or hiding accomplishments. This can come in many forms, like revealing some hurt or fear or hardship that you are having and inflating it or exaggerating your reaction to the stress to make you look unstable. In addition, not sharing your success with family members in an attempt to further the idea that you are unstable, incompetent, or that he is carrying the load for you is another tactic. Remember, when dealing with the narcissist, there is only room for one success story in the family, and that space is reserved for him.

Case Study No. 5. "When I retired, I kept asking him when he is going to tell his mother because it was definitely a cause for celebration. He kept telling me he did not want to tell her because he did not want her to worry about our finances. I said it's a retirement. It is not like I got fired. He finally said he would not tell her and insisted that I should not tell her or she would worry."

Gaslighting and Verbal Abuse

Gaslighting and verbal abuse are the all-time favorites of the narcissist, convincing you or others of a false view of a memory, especially of some pain that he caused. If he gets desperate to get a reaction out of you—because he will need you to fight with him to set up his discard—he will resort to verbal abuse. All this is in an effort to control you and to make you feel inferior and/or confused. That is because by this stage, he is realizing that you are uncovering the true person behind the mask—flaws, insecurities, hypocrisy, and all—or he has found another victim to love-bomb. In some extreme cases, physical abuse will and can occur during this time. "All narcissists will abuse whether mental, physical, sexual, or spiritual. You may be thinking, 'My partner does not hit me, so maybe he or she is not narcissistic. All narcissists are psychologically and emotionally abusive. Some are physical or sexual abusers as well. Sociopaths and psychopaths are narcissistic at the core of their being."[9]

Case Study No. 1. "When I finally spoke with his ex-wife, she told me about the horrible physical abuse that she endured. She said she was tired of the abuse. Of course, he painted a picture of being a supportive husband and leaving her in a position to care for herself and the children."

Case Study No. 4. "He was controlling my dress, my hair, even what I ate. He was always looking at other women and comparing me to them, which caused me to have low self-esteem. I thought I couldn't find anyone else. Our lifestyle catered around his sexual desires. He always said I could stop, but he would never let me. I continued to cater to his lifestyle out of manipulation and fear of being alone."

Case Study No. 5. "The last week of our marriage, he created a lot of chaos. He started an argument each day about the smallest things: my being at the hospital with family, my turning down a job, my spending time looking for a building for our religious community, my organization of his event. It was me, me, me. In one instance, I went into the bedroom to get away from his ranting, and he followed me. I tried to close the door so my son would not hear the ranting. He kept blocking the door with his foot, kicking it open. I was told that he was this way in a previous marriage, ranting periodically like clockwork, inconsolable every few months. He and I never argued the entire marriage. Three years, eleven months, and three weeks of love-bombing with sprinkles of sabotage and backhanded compliments. Then the last week of the marriage, he was like Dr. Jekyll and Mr. Hyde, and then he was gone."

---

[9]   Karyl McBride, *Will I Ever Be Free of You?* (2015).

Provoking

The narcissist is an expert at provoking you then blaming you for the argument. This is a very common tactic so he can become the victim on any given day. He will also use this tactic during the abandonment or discard so he can point to the conflict as the reason for the abandonment. Provoking is also a way to distract you from what he is doing or planning to do. If he knows you well, he will also know your weak spots, insecurities, and/or common triggers. Sometimes the narcissist will provoke you just as a "check-in" to see if he still has your attention emotionally and can get under your skin. Whether good or bad, he wants your attention because this gives him some evidence of control over you and/or your emotions and will make him feel important. These little tests will also help him plan the chaos that will lead to the abandonment.

Blame Shifting

Finally, there is blame shifting, which is the ultimate tactic. His acts of deception, aggression, demeaning, physical abuse, abuse of prescription and/or street drugs, indulgence in hidden addictions such as pornography or homosexuality will be because of *you*. Whatever harm or transgressions he inflicts is because you made him do it as if he had absolutely no part in it, no control over it, and no willpower of his own. When he finally abandons, *you* will be the reason. The narcissist will take his blame shifting all the way to the pearly gates where he will blame his wives, children, and parents for all his devilment and then demand entry into paradise!

Case Study No. 2. "He gets a suspicious phone call. When I question him, he goes into a tirade and says we don't need to do this [move into the new house] and that it's my fault for starting the argument. Now we won't be moving into the house that I already had the loan for and the movers and had given up my place. He asks for his portion of the money back! I refused. He said if I didn't return the money, we cannot be anything in the future. I moved into the house alone. He was supposed to pay half the mortgage. Now it was a financial struggle for me. I finally sold the house after living there for almost two years."

Case Study No. 5. "He never once gave me any reason for the abandonment. He told my uncle that I was physically aggressive to him, and he left because he didn't want to hit me, but my uncle shut that down as a lie. He never once stated this in court. I assume it would have saved him from paying spousal support if he had stated this to the judge while he was on the stand. I have never tried to fight anyone, man or woman, in my life. His only objection to the spousal support was that my income was higher, but I would think that a threatening or physically combative spouse would be a good out."

The narcissist is a controlled time bomb, always ticking with a smile on his face. At the root of all his behaviors is fear, because being a con artist is a 24/7, 365-day job that never lets up, and each step must be calculated. The problem is that he is an emotional criminal, and like any criminal, he is prone to mistakes. He is not the "smartest person in the room" as he will try to brainwash you to believe. Make no mistake. In very extreme cases, the malignant narcissist—unlike the white-knight narcissist—will try to physically harm you. That is because the malignant narcissist goes beyond their self-absorbing behavior and the need to be held in high regard by others. The malignant narcissist will be highly manipulative and will not stop at hurting others—even physically—to get his way. The white-knight narcissist is self-absorbed much like the malignant narcissist; however, he will infuse himself in families, communities, and/or activities that will allow him to be seen as charitable or giving and will use this as a cover to manipulate others.

Remember the cycle: He will love-bomb you with affection and gifts. Next, he will demean you to lower your self-esteem or make you feel responsible for his bad behavior, then create and escalate arguments disproportionate to the situation. He will become distant and ignore you with the silent treatment. After that, he may offer a half-hearted apology, which, for the narcissist, may simply mean breaking his silence, or he will play the victim, extracting an apology from you and start the process again. It will be so subtle that you will not notice the process at first. In fact, if he is a really manipulative, high-functioning narcissist, you may not notice the process at all until it's too late. He will run the smear campaign and use this as his reason for the abandonment. All his actions and thoughts are for immediate self-gratification. When that ends, he will use any obstacle in the relationship as a reason to eventually abandon for someone new. He will always want to be in the "love-bombing" stage, where he is glorified. This is because he also seeks to constantly control and dominate others, so the ultimate satisfaction is being in a position of authority and admiration.

Case Study No. 4. "When he manipulated me into this lifestyle that catered to his sexual desires, he promised me that at any time, either of us could say stop and we would stop. There were many times I asked to stop, but he never did. His controlling me also showed up with him being controlling of my eating, working out, my dress, hairstyles, etc."

Stage 3—Abandonment/Discard

If you were not sure that your husband or significant other was/is a narcissist before now, this stage, abandonment, is the evidence. While some narcissists will continue to cycle you through stages 1 (love-bombing) and 2 (spirit-breaking) for the duration of a long-term relationship, according to Keithley Law, PLLC, "The narcissist's discard—throwing away—of the family is the *clearest sign* that your spouse suffered from narcissism." He goes on to explain that he uses the term *narcissism* interchangeably with every other cluster B psychopathology that includes but is not limited to antisocial and borderline personality disorder. He explains that one of the reasons that a narcissist will pull a disappearing act is because "the narcissist is self-centered, entitled, and believes it is beneath him to owe you an explanation." Narcissists are not cut from the same cloth as us. They simply don't want to be bothered by you, and a marriage to them is no different than a casual hookup. They will block your calls and block you on social media, and they will receive an ego boost when you attempt to contact them for an explanation.[10]

Case Study No. 5. "My husband left my son and me on our anniversary vacation two states away and did not answer his phone, I only called him once. I then emailed him to document the conversation, and I asked him to explain his actions. He said, 'I won't bother to explain it to you because you wouldn't understand.' I never received an explanation. He never even bothered to explain it to my father, who was living with us and whom he claimed to love. My father passed away six weeks later with no word of condolence from my husband. We were never able to convince my father that this abandonment didn't have anything to do with him."

The abandonment will be precalculated. Oftentimes, the wife will not be aware that anything has changed as the "dutiful husband" stage play that supports his manufactured life is still ongoing. There will be no discussion of any issues or problems to resolve because alerting you to legitimate or imagined problems in the marriage or staying in the marriage is not the goal. The intent, as it has been since stage 1 (love-bombing), is to leave without warning, not to repair and/or grow the marriage. Once the narcissist knows you have seen behind the mask he's wearing; that you realize he is not at all what

---

[10] Keithley Law, "Why Do Narcissists Pull Disappearing Acts?" (August 2019), keithleylaw.com/blog/.

he presents; that hypocrisy, deceit, and bullying are at his very core, he will run!

In a last-ditch effort, he may stage a huge unexpected argument as part of the exit. He may not even bother with this extra step. He will have to stage this because, in all probability, since he has been playing the role of the happy, dutiful husband, this is going to be a 180-degree turn. He may use multiple scenarios. For example, he may come home and announce he wants a divorce and walk out for good. You may come home to find him packed up and gone, or you may go on your honeymoon where you find yourself abandoned. In other scenarios, he may come home and announce he wants a divorce and tell you to pack your bags! As unbelievable as all these scenarios sound, they are very real occurrences that you will see from some of the women who were interviewed for this book. Either way, he will, without warning, move on to reinvent himself and restart stage 1 (love-bombing) with a new victim. It is extremely important to recognize this process because it is only then that you can protect yourself, children, and family. When you see the process, the fog is lifted, and you can make sense of what is happening to you and those around you.

Case Study No. 1. "After he proposed, I told him that he had to meet with my mother. We set a date and time to meet with her. On that day, a couple hours prior, I texted him to confirm. He said we would have to do it another time. I asked him when, what day, and time. He didn't respond. I never heard from him again. I saw him at another masjid, and he ignored me. I later learned he had done this numerous times, even going as far as having the women look for new apartments then abandoning the engagement."

Case Study No. 2. "The week that we were supposed to move into the home that we purchased together, I questioned him about a telephone call. He blew up, immediately creating a huge argument, saying that we were not going to be able to move into the home. He wanted the down payment back, but I refused. We did not move into the home together. I moved into the home alone."

Case Study No. 3. "He came back for a week. While he was there, he created all this chaos and confusion. There was a big argument, and that was his excuse to leave. He always tried to manipulate the situation and make it seem like I started the argument so he would have an excuse to leave. The abandonment really started right after the wedding, on the honeymoon."

Case Study No. 4. "He began spending a lot of time with a female colleague from his work. He claimed that he was helping her study. I had no idea this was coming. I was trying my hardest to do whatever I could for my husband. I knew about him studying with the coworker, and I was fairly accommodating to his request to go and study with her. I felt like he had his cake and was eating it too, so why would he ever ask for a divorce? Then out of nowhere, he said he wanted a divorce."

Case Study No. 5. "We went away on a family vacation that was also our wedding anniversary. Just two days before, he had given me a card in which he wrote, 'Alhamdulillah [all praise to God], and thank you for four beautiful years of marriage.' So I was not at all aware of what he was planning. We arrived on Friday that night, and he was unusually quiet. He was very preoccupied. Saturday morning, he said he was going home and we need to separate. He picked up a suitcase that was already surprisingly packed, then he left us in the hotel two states away, still in our pajamas. He had removed us from our home, took us away, and left in a prearranged rental car. When I texted to ask where he had parked my vehicle, he took six hours to respond. I was sick on what was supposed to be our anniversary trip and couldn't comprehend how the person who said he loved me two days before would be so cruel to me and to my son. I pushed my feeling deep down to protect my son."

You may ask, How can any man who claims to be God-fearing do this? The point is to control and humiliate, to feel a sense of power over you. Dr. Linda Martinez-Lewi explains that for the narcissist, there are no true commitments except to his own self-satisfaction. Family members—wives, children, even parents—are disposable. He will not look back because, in discard, the goal is to get as far away as possible.

It may seem that he is running from the family; however, he is also running from himself and the reality of his own fears of inadequacy or running to indulge in some mental or physical addiction or alternate lifestyle. With the family alienation and smear campaign completed in stage 2 (demeaning and spirit-breaking), he hopes that there will be no one to come to your aid. In fact, he is relying on your previous praise of him in stage 1 (love-bombing) to cause others to doubt you now. Even more so, he is relying on your silence to pave the way for him to rinse and repeat this process with the next victim.

Sandra L. Brown, founder of the Institute for Relational Harm Reduction and Public Pathology Education, says that over 60 million persons in the US have been negatively affected and/or abused by someone exhibiting this type of pathology. She goes on to explain that "recovery is both action oriented and awareness based. But if awareness is not leading you to action, you are stuck in your recovery process and need help to change gears."[11]

The narcissists will create a tornado of confusion, uncertainty, and anxiety. You will look back and try to piece all the deception together and wonder how you missed all the signs. After abandonment, you may ask yourself, "Was I too trusting? Did I fit a profile?" The answer is yes and no.

You may be Muslim, Christian, Jewish, atheist—it does not matter. There is no set profile for the victim of this type of abuse except that you had some quality, reputation, material possessions, or just physical attributes that would benefit him in some way. In other words, a good cover, met his physical needs, and/or good arm candy so he can keep up appearances as a family man while living a life of deception. You were simply in the right or wrong place at the right time for him to rob you of your emotional security and trust in the human spirit!

Please know that it has nothing to do with you and everything to do with the broken person that is him. This is who he is. This is what he does. This is what he will continue to do.

---

[11] Sandra Brown, "Awareness Is Not Enough," Institute for Relational Harm Reduction and Public Pathology Education Newsletter (2022).

Case Study No. 4. "I stayed downstairs in the kitchen, seriously contemplating suicide. I even had a knife to my wrist. I believe God spoke to me to put the knife down. I was scared, so I went up to tell him what had just happened. I told him I needed him to hold me. He replied, 'You selfish b——. I can't believe you would even think of killing yourself. What would Shae, our daughter, and I do? I can't even look at you right now, let alone touch you!'"

If you are a victim of abandonment, doing just a small amount of investigation will likely reveal that you were not his first victim, nor will you be his last. He will usually have multiple overlapping uncommitted relationships, broken engagements and/or marriages, and even long-term marriages that were plagued with manipulation, a secret lifestyle, and/or infidelity. His actions may be revealed accidentally due to his arrogance and because in the past, his behavior has gone undetected and/or unchallenged. This is the boiler-plate narcissistic love-abuse-abandon cycle as the process never changes. The narcissists will target the victim; love-bomb with extreme interest, gifts, and/or affection; devalue and demean; and then abandon/discard. This is the ugly truth and is not at all condoned in any religion or civilized community.

Al-Bukhari and Muslim reported, "A Muslim is a brother for another Muslim, and he/she does not wrong them or abandon them..." (Source Hadith: Ṣaḥīḥ al-Bukhārī 2422, Ṣaḥīḥ Muslim 2580).

Case Study No. 1. "After he ghosted the engagement, I learned that he had done this numerous times. I also learned that he had been extremely abusive—mentally and physically—to his previous wife. She talked about the year of abuse she suffered and that she was tired of taking the abuse and that although he had several degrees and a practice, that he did not provide for the family financially."

Case Study No. 2. "He was addicted to sex. He had told me about his ex-wife, saying he must go to counseling for this addiction. He said she was crazy, but I knew that this was an addiction for him. No matter what you do for them, they will not be able to overcome this addiction. There is nothing you can do to help this."

Case Study No. 3. "When it was all exposed, he was still in the life of crime, he was still into drugs, he was still engaged in sexual relationships, he was still engaged in all those things even though he talked about them as if they were in the past. Because of the way he presented his life, I also treated those things as if they were in the past, but he talked about it so much. That was a red flag."

Case Study No. 4. "Manipulation around the sex in our marriage was very pervasive. The fact that he seemed more interested in other women really tore down my self-esteem. The times he left my three-year-old daughter and me while he went to be with his female coworker really hurt me emotionally."

Case Study No. 5. "The morning after our wedding, he told me about extreme substance abuse that included multiple overdoses. At first, I didn't believe it because he was currently a very accomplished professional. I asked him how he overcome such extreme addiction. He said, 'I just decided to stop.' This made no sense, but it was the morning after our wedding, and I didn't want to ruin it with more questions or by accusing him of lying. After my abandonment, I learned that he divulged this same information to a previous wife during his abrupt abandonment from their marriage."

CHAPTER 4

Revealing the Link Between Narcissism and Abandonment

And when I am ill, it is He who cures me.
(Holy Quran Surah Ash-Shu'ara 26:80)

I waited patiently for the LORD; he turned to me and heard my cry. He lifted me out of the slimy pit, out of the mud and mire; he set my feet on a rock and gave me a firm place to stand. (Psalm 40: 1–31)

I saw a lecture by an Imam/Minister explaining how some believe that mental health disorders are the result of not fully practicing the religion or being weak in your faith. Many years ago, there was the belief that mental health disorders were some sort of possession by an evil spirit. This can lead to the idea that increasing your practice, faith in God, prayers, and reciting religious scriptures will eliminate these illnesses. While this can be a remedy for increasing your fortitude and faith that will help you to overcome many obstacles in life, suffering from mental or physical illness or addictions is not evidence of disbelief and may actually require a medical or psychological practitioner.

Narcissism is a mental health condition that we have heard a great deal about over the last few years. The term has been used loosely and incorrectly to explain a host of undesirable behaviors. "Narcissistic Personality Disorder is a mental illness and one of several types of personality disorders. It is a mental condition in which the person has an inflated sense of their own importance and a deep need for excessive attention and admiration."[12]

Even when the narcissist is giving attention to others, it serves the purpose of bringing attention to himself. Obtaining this attention or affection will never be enough because the overwhelming need for new attention, affection, and admiration will always lead to a string of troubled relationships with spouses, family, friends, and even colleagues. Narcissists need constant praise, and each new spouse or relationship is really just a temporary distraction until he becomes dissatisfied once again and moves on to a new distraction.

This strong need can cause him to have no empathy or concern for how his actions affect others. Behind this mask of bravado is a fragile self-esteem that needs to be fueled with constant attention and positive affirmation and reinforcement. The narcissist is much like a parasite and needs you, the host, in order to survive. Narcissists will feed off your love of life, your spirit, and your soul! He will drain you mentally, physically, emotionally, and financially, and then he will move on to the next host! If you are lucky, he will move on before you have been completely destroyed.

---

[12] Mayo Clinic, Mayo Foundation for Medical Education and Research (MFMER) (1998–2022), www.mayoclinic.org/diseases-conditions/narcissistic-personality-disorder.

"People with narcissistic personality disorder may not want to think that anything could be wrong, so they are unlikely to seek treatment. If individuals do seek treatment, it's more likely to be for symptoms of depression, drug or alcohol use, or another mental health problem. But perceived insults to self-esteem may make it difficult to accept and follow through with treatment."[13] Due to his inflated ego and belief that he is the smartest person in the room, he will attempt to use his uncanny ability of deception to deceive the therapist as well. If he cannot successfully deceive the therapist, he will likely deem the therapist incompetent or he will rage and reject therapy altogether.

This is all very complicated, but I am sure by now you can think of someone that you have encountered at home, work, school, or in your religious community that has these narcissistic traits or behaviors and perhaps even an official diagnosis. Diagnosis or not, if you spot these behaviors, you should keep a safe emotional and possible physical distance from this personality type.

"Narcissistic relationships are transactional, by transactional, I mean that the narcissist likes you and want you around when you serve their needs. They lose interest in you when you do not. No matter how much they claim to love you, the reality is that it is not you, the individual, that they love. They love the functions you perform for them."[14] These functions can be mental, physical, financial, and/or spiritual. The narcissist will drain you from every angle, and they are always looking for the next host to support their needs.

If you have encountered a narcissist, it is very likely that their account of their childhood is full of examples of how they were misunderstood, neglected, or treated unfairly when, in fact, it could be they were often overpraised in an effort to console them.

Psychologist, Elinor Greenberg, explains that narcissists lack whole object relations, meaning that he will see people as *all* good or *all* bad and he cannot form an integrated view of an individual. She explains that "this leads to people with NPD to be hyper-focused on

---

[13]   Mayo Clinic, "Narcissistic Personality Disorder."

[14]   Elinor Greenberg, *Psychology Today*, ed., Vanessa Lancaster (March 2022).

projecting an image that they feel is admirable and blameless. It also leads them to devaluing other people or not taking responsibility for their share of failures and faults."[15]

Perhaps this is how one goes from being love-bombed to demeaned in a blink of an eye. It seems that the narcissist will idealize you or despise you; there is no in between. He will be hyperfocused on any reduction in your accolades, idolization, or adoration of him. With any slip up, you chance quickly falling from the pedestal on which he has placed you. That is because you are not on this pedestal for you but for him. He has placed you on this pedestal to make a display of his supposed love for you or as a reward for your adoration of him. Either way, it is to advance his counterfeit persona. If you should see behind his mask of deception or his true insecurities, you become disposable and damaged goods. You have, in fact, assaulted his ego by having the audacity to see his deceptions.

You don't have to be a doctor to recognize all the ways he can bring narcissistic destruction to your life. He does not have to be formally diagnosed with narcissistic personality disorder. For example, a person with a nasty cold or flu does not need a formal diagnosis for you to see that they are sick or can spread the illness. It is clear from the person's symptoms and the actual infection spreading from person to person that the person is sick. When you see that someone is sick with a cold or the flu, you instinctively keep your distance and maybe wear a mask. That person may be instructed to stay home from work and limit contact to prevent infecting others. If you live with that person, you may start to take vitamins to strengthen your immune system. Likewise, if you recognize the symptoms of narcissism (lack of empathy, self-gratification, attention-seeking, manipulation, etc.) and the spread of the disease (destruction of lives, marriage hopping, addictive behaviors, and psychological or physical abuse), you should take the same precautions! Keep your distance and build your support system! You don't need a formal diagnosis to take commonsense precautions; however, a diagnosis by a trained health-care

---

[15] Elinor Greenberg, "Understanding Narcissism: How Can Narcissists Claim to Be Both Heroes and Victims?" (November 20, 2021).

professional is what can hopefully lead to meaningful treatment. The narcissists will likely resist, but you can get treatment for yourself so you can protect yourself from or rid yourself of the narcissist.

Be aware that the more you try to protect yourself from the narcissist, the harder he will play the victim as he is quite skilled at deception. When is a known narcissist lying? Always! If he is talking, even in his sleep, he is lying. He can also be quite intimidating and back you off from calling out his lies. Once you do, he will become privately enraged, but not publicly, because playing the victim helps him achieve his overall goal of abuse without guilt. Since narcissists typically lack empathy or have no desire to feel empathy, it makes lack of remorse very easy. In addition, the feeling of entitlement and overexaggerated self-worth fuel the notion that they are entitled to wipe their feet on you, and you should say, "Thank you!"

The narcissist will use you up mentally, physically, spiritually, and financially, then abandon and destroy everything in his path, deploying the scorched-earth maneuver while he is leaving. Everything in his wake will be destroyed. But you can still be a formidable opponent if you do not allow him to be the source from which you gain your spiritual and emotional strength. It will be a major blow; however, it is survivable. You might ask yourself, "Do these people know right from wrong?" Yes, they are well aware of right from wrong; however, they work extremely hard to justify everything that they do to make you or someone else the problem and themselves the victim.

> Al-Nu'man ibn Bashir reported, the Messenger of Allah, peace and blessings be upon him, said: Verily, in the body is a piece of flesh which, if sound, the entire body is sound, and if corrupt, the entire body is corrupt. Truly, it is the heart. (Ṣaḥīḥ al-Bukhārī Book 22 Hadith 133)

Imagine it's Thanksgiving Day. There's a perfectly browned turkey! But as you carve into the turkey, you notice that it's not completely done. You and your family keep eating, ignoring those parts that are not done because, well...it's Thanksgiving Day, and no one wants to ruin Thanksgiving Day! So you all keep eating. You all get sick! Everyone is saying, "I knew it wasn't quite done, but I just couldn't ruin everyone's excitement over the turkey!" The thing that's not quite right with the narcissist is that he is missing *true* sincerity, empathy, compassion, honesty, and integrity. He is giving you his counterfeit persona and his manufactured life. People know something is off, but since it's rare to come across this strange bird, they just can't identify the problem or, in this case, the danger. Many people, in hindsight, will say that they thought or felt that something was not quite right, but they just couldn't put their finger on it. Afterward, they will recount all the missing links, stories that didn't add up, reactions that were not socially acceptable, outbursts that were not justified, or affection that was inappropriate to the spouse or others in the family or even strangers.

Case Study No. 2. "There is always going to be something that's off [with the narcissist], something that's just not quite right. If you meet someone and constantly find yourself saying 'Who *does* that?' or 'Who *says* that?' or 'Who *behaves* that way?' please get far away!"

Case Study No. 4. "There were many things that didn't feel good about the relationship, some things that actually scared me, but I had it in my mind that I needed to get married and that he was supposed to be my husband. I didn't believe I could actually make it on my own, and I didn't know how else I would meet someone, because at that time, I had low self-esteem. I had a feeling in me that if I just loved him enough, I could change whatever didn't feel right and everything would work out. He slow-walked the manipulation, taking me down a dark and slippery slope over nine years."

Case Study No. 5. "I did feel things were going fast, and I felt a bit of pressure. He mentioned marriage during our first conversation. However, I soon got swept up in the possibilities when he continuously talked about his work and books on boys who had absentee fathers and how he could be a support system for my son. This was the promise that sealed the deal for me. I was a divorced single mother, and a positive male influence for my son and his proclamation of being a practicing Muslim, seemed desirable. I later learned that this was not his first time using this angle."

In addition, the narcissist is methodical and will manipulate and control your emotions, constantly writing and revising the script. He is playing a role on a stage, and everyone around him is a puppet on a string. He has gone into the relationship aware of his intent and will not change his behavior from the previous marriage or relationship because this is what works for him. His goal, first and foremost, is to be in control of every step, large or small, and this includes controlling *your* behavior as well. If he is well, the family is well, Since the narcissist seeks to write and control the narrative of all those around him. If he is in a bad mood, he will manipulate the entire family into a bad mood. Everyone will walk on eggshells, waiting for his mood to change. Then suddenly, he will make a grand gesture of breaking the silence or he will purchase lavish gifts or treat the family to something special. The lavish gifts or surprisingly good treatment or special outing are to put him back in the adoration phase all while planning the next downward spiral. Rinse, repeat… rinse, repeat…rinse, repeat.

As the wife, you are a puppet in this manipulative process. You will be the person that strokes and fuels his ego. Nevertheless, he will make you the cause of his misery or target of his hate, and finally, you will become his excuse for abandonment. Love, demean, abandon—rinse and repeat, rinse and repeat. The wife and sometimes even the children are simply "beards" or props he will "throw away" after his performance is over. Sometimes, in the case of the children, he will shower them with material possessions to buy affection and adoration.

Dr. Martinez-Lewis explains that male narcissists are often controlled by their mothers. "Momma, mom, mother adored them to use as her puppet and her psychological partner. She chose her son over her husband. Some adult male narcissists report that mother comes to visit the family and in secret tells her son that she wants to go to dinner with him for a 'date.' The narcissistic male is often psychologically possessed by his mother. Unconsciously he grows to hate her. There is always an ambivalence with mother, a love/hate relationship. The male child cannot be free and is emasculated."[16]

If he has managed to obtain some perceived success professionally, in the religious community, or in the family, he will use this as a shield to hide his deceptive behavior. He will count on using religion, reputation, money, or educational status to cover his true intent. He will use this to manipulate everyone around you to make himself the victim and you the villain. He will say that he is far above the things that you accuse him of and that someone with his stature—such as a PhD or an attorney, teacher, economic status, or a medical doctor—would not behave in this way, and he is partially right. Those who are of the highest education levels in society typically are seen as leaders and responsible for the educational, ethical, and humanitarian progression of society. Please be aware that there is an ethical code of conduct at some universities that goes along with being conferred with PhDs that they must uphold honesty, integrity, trustworthiness, loyalty, fairness, concern and respect for others, and be law-abiding. But put degrees and money aside, how do you truly measure success?

He will never be responsible for any wrongdoing. He will say, "She made me do it because..." then accuse her of physical aggression, emotional abuse, or being emotionally unstable or emotionally absent. He may also say she became a drinker or a drug user or she was flirting with other men or some other evil conjured up by him that instigated his abusive or immoral act. Again, check his track record. Which of these excuses did he use to discredit previous wives and/or significant others? He will use whatever reason that seems excusable to the person he's addressing, but if you check, he will likely have used a different reason with each person. Whatever excuse will be jaw-dropping to your family and friends, his current target, or those in the new target's sphere of protection. The narcissist will never meet an excuse that he does not like!

---

[16] Linda Martinez-Lewis, "Narcissistic Men Despise Independent Women" (October 15, 2012).

Case Study No. 3. "He told me that his ex was crazy. She did seem to be unstable. I soon realized that it was him that made her that way."

Case Study No. 5. "He told my brother-in-law that his ex was an alcoholic and that was why he left her. He never told me that. He told me that the marriage was a result of his grief from the passing of previous spouse, so they mutually agreed to separate. I learned that this was not true. He abruptly left their marriage."

This form of victim blaming does not come without precedent. Assault victims, like victims of abandonment, are often blamed for the violence. For example, after physical or sexual assault, unfortunately sometimes the first questions are, "What was *she* wearing?" "Was *she* out at night?" as if this justifies the assault with no questions about the rapist. In the case of abandonment, these types of questions are also asked: "What did *she* do to provoke him?" "Was *she* ignoring his needs?" He will capitalize on this thought process to avoid accountability as he blames the victim, sometimes in elaborate detail, saying that the victim did to him what he *knows* he did to her. This attempt to rewrite the facts, to change the public view of what has occurred is called gaslighting and is used to create confusion about who the real victim and perpetrator are. The narcissist is an expert at playing the victim even while simultaneously being an abuser, mentally and/or physically.

Case Study No. 1. "When I let the wakil know that I was concerned about some things I had heard about my intended, he was appalled...with *me*! He said I was slandering him and backbiting him. He told me not to listen to women who are not married because they are jealous. The wakil was dismissive of me each time and didn't believe me until after the abandonment."

Case Study No. 2. "His family thought very highly of him and would cover for him in his deceptions. To them, he walked on water."

Case Study No. 3. "A lot of people talked me out of my conflicting thoughts. They said such things as 'You know, he probably needs a place to vent.' 'You know, he probably never had someone listen to him.'"

Case Study No. 4. "Most people don't believe that abandonment and desertion occur, unless they spend some time learning about the dynamics of the narcissistic relationship."

Like any abusive relationship, many people will say "Why did *you* let it happen? I would have been out of there a long time ago" or even "I don't know why *you* didn't see what was going on." Many times, hearing things like these retraumatizes the victim.

In the relationship, the gaslighting was designed to make the victim question their own reality. Innocently, family and friends can retrigger those feelings of not being heard or believed.

Case Study No. 5. "I was told by his family member that I was not abandoned because I had my own car when he left us two states away. His family member said 'Well, sometimes people get frustrated' in response to me calling to say he had abandoned me and my son on our vacation and I didn't know where he was. I quickly began to suspect that she knew his plans or had seen him do this before because she did not seem surprised. I also had the feeling that if I had called to say that he blackened my eye, they would have advised me to stop running into his fist. It was useless. The only members of his family that showed sympathy were those that did not have the power to hold him accountable."

The narcissist's control is not always immediate or blatant. It will come in stages, and people may ask you how you allowed this behavior. However, initially, he will be at your beck and call during the love-bombing stage. He will gradually pull back, and for a time, it will seem you are equally serving each other. Then soon you find yourself stifling your own spirit, growth, or wants and needs to avoid the silent treatments, physical distancing, passive-aggressive behavior, or even rage. This is possibly the first level of control the narcissist will inflict on you, suppressing your wants, needs, and emotions. So your question may be, "If he is so bad, how did he, at one time, treat me so good?" I will give a direct answer to this question and how this affects the family, wife, and religious community in the next chapter.

CHAPTER 5

Hidden Dangers for the Family and Community

The question in the previous chapter was, "If he is so bad, how did he, at one time, treat me so good?" These can coexist. At first, he does really enjoy your company during the love-bombing stage. However, he doesn't enjoy it in the sense of mutual appreciation and affection from which you enjoy the relationship. He enjoys you during the love-bombing stage because it's at that point you are most oblivious to his deception. He enjoys your company because you are freely giving your love, devotion, and admiration, as a wife should. This will also inflate his ego for onlookers. You are oblivious to the red flags that this is not genuinely reciprocated. He will reciprocate only as a means of control. The narcissist will use religion, love, protection, emotional support, gifts, affection, money, or even sex to manipulate or control the victim in stage 1 (love-bombing) and then systematically take these away in stage 2 (demeaning/spirit-breaking). You will see evidence of all these in the case studies presented in this book.

That "good treatment" comes from a specific type of narcissist according to psychologist Elinor Greenberg. She describes two types of narcissists: the malignant narcissist, which is the dictator type, and then there is the "white-knight narcissist."[17] The white-knight narcissist will seek out his supply/victim in places where he can be seen as altruistic or charitable. He can still be self-centered and even cruel when you are alone, but he will conceal these undesirable traits with public good/acceptable behavior. If he is caught in the act of his cruelty, he will lean on this good public behavior and beseech those around him to remember all his well-placed public acts of kindness to counter any slip-ups.

When caught in the act or exposed, he will say things like, "But you know me... I am [insert profession/degree/title/role/charitable action/income status]. *You know me.*" But this is just his counterfeit persona, the role that he plays. He will do this because he knows that most people will not challenge the ever-cunning and deceitful narcissist who can also be an intimidating, raging, violent person if necessary and if he thinks he can get away with it. Unfortunately, he will have manipulated family and friends to ensure that you have no support. He will unleash them on you to keep his hands clean. Some of them are victims of his manipulation as you were, while others have been coddling him and excusing his behavior since childhood. Friends and colleagues view him as successful, therefore overlook his arrogance and sometimes bully-like behavior.

Case Study No. 2. "He asked one of his friends if I were coming to his father's funeral [because our families have been close since childhood]. He was still making attempts to see me. He was still trying to reach out to me through friends. If I knew he was going to be somewhere I would potentially be, I made sure to not be there. He continued to pursue me, and I continued to be unavailable. I

---

17 Elinor Greenberg, "White Knights and Black Knights: Prosocial and Antisocial NPD" (2014).

was finally free of him after many years of manipulation. I took my power back."

Case Study No. 5. "Almost two months after the abandonment, his family member called and said that he left us because I was paying more attention to the kids than to him on our vacation. This seemed to justify for her, leaving us two states away, going home, and clearing it of all his belongings while we slept unaware. He gave at least four different unrelated reasons for his actions to different family members but never to me. Much like he gave multiple reasons for his previous divorces that didn't match. I had learned by this time that he would provide whatever reason would be acceptable to each person. She literally ended the conversation with 'He don't want you! Nah, nah, nah!' I was shocked by this immature behavior by an elder over a very adult issue that devastated my son. I was also shocked because up until the abandonment, she had ended every conversation with "Love you!" even just one week before. A light switch was turned off on that love that was conditional it seemed only he loved me too. I was in the twilight zone!"

The term coined for those who knowingly and unknowingly support the narcissist's abusive behavior is *flying monkeys.* It comes from the movie the *Wizard of Oz*; however, it is meant to describe those sent out to do the bidding of the manipulator. Believe it or not, the spouse is for a time unknowingly one of the *flying monkeys*! Think about it, you will remember during the love-bombing and sometimes the demeaning stage that you supported him because he said he was misunderstood, disrespected, or not fully acknowledged for his worth by those around him. He filled your head with all the ways his family, friends, and colleagues were simply jealous of him that he had education, power, money, material possessions, looks, or even because he had *you*! These same family members will defend him and try to torment you. Another example is the lies he will undoubtedly tell you about a previous spouse and/or relationship. He will seem to have no fault in the demise. It will be so extreme and detailed that you would think, *Who can make that up? Your* belief in him puts you in the realm of a flying monkey, doing his bidding, believing, defending, supporting, and feeling empathy for him.

It is at the very moment you become aware of the lies and hypocrisy that you stop being a flying monkey and become a liability. That's when he will dive deep into stage 2 (demeaning and spirit-breaking) and set up for stage 3 (abandonment/discard), the disappearing act. Although he is emotionally a child in an adult's body, this is by no means child's play because lives are indeed at stake. The narcissist is a con artist at heart and well-versed in manipulation and will wreak havoc in all aspects of your life.

Family and friends being manipulated may have no idea they are part of the con. For example, you may hear from a friend or family member who has until this point been absent. They will call you to check on you before, during, or maybe even after his abandonment. They may say things like "He did not want me to call you" or "I did not tell him that I was going to call you" to try to gain your trust. They, too, have been manipulated and will try to gauge your emotional state to report back to the narcissist. This is, in essence, the act of deploying *flying monkeys*.

The narcissist will attempt to use everything against you, the victim—family, friends, community members, colleagues, and even the religion. He will be unscrupulous in his attempt to use every imaginable tactic to take support away from you. This will be done in an attempt to compromise any safe space that you will try to retreat to for protection or support. Even your most immediate family members will be an attempted weapon.

Case Study No. 5. "He made multiple attempts to discredit me to my own family. None of his attempts worked. He even tried to get me to blame myself for his behavior. He responded to my email when I arrived home to find him cleared out, that all my family was against me and talking about me to him. I did not fall for this flimsy attempt to sabotage my confidence in my family."

The narcissist's unscrupulous spirit and uncanny ability to lie will seem *almost* impenetrable, because he was planning ahead and you are now working behind the 8-ball. He had already planned and completed the smear campaign on your character while you were in stage 2 (spirit-breaking and demeaning) and living unknowingly in his smoke-screened manufactured life. If you allow him, he will try and plant doubt in your head that he did not do this or that you did this to yourself or, even worse, that you did this to *him*. He is an expert at running the "love-bomb-demean-love-bomb" process and will try to use this to make you and anyone in earshot doubt what he has done. This will look like the love-bombing stage, but now he will run this tired play in reverse. If he realizes that you are now "woke," he will double down and he will continue to attack your character, so don't "get ready…stay ready" and stay prayed up! The only thing that can defeat a lie is the *truth*, so speak out and do not let him continue to hide in plain sight!

You must courageously and openly call out the abuse! Do not let him or fear make you an enemy of yourself. Do not be afraid. Allah/God is always with you. Allah/God will send guardians—seen and unseen—to flank you on your right and your left, in front and behind. Sometimes He will even make you undetectable while you make necessary moves to recover and allow you to see what was not supposed to be seen by you. Flying monkeys have no power over the protection of the wings of angels! You will find the suggestions and recommendations on how to call out the abuse later in the chapter "Reclaiming Your Life!"

Remember, the innocent man stays, while the guilty man flees. If he professes to be a Muslim, remarrying a Muslim or a non-Muslim will be easy. This is because marriage is the expectation of all Muslims. Marriage is considered half of your religious obligation, and true Muslim men have a good reputation for being committed to family and religious and community life. Other men of faith will also use this tactic; therefore, religion is a perfect cover for them. He will exploit the religion, the community, his family, and of course, your honest desire for marriage to complete your religious obligations to maintain his counterfeit persona that defines him as a person.

> In their hearts is a disease, so Allah has increased their disease; and for them is a painful punishment because they [habitually] used to lie. (Quran 2:10)

There is nothing concealed that will not be disclosed or hidden that will not be made known. (The Holy Bible, Luke 12:2)

The Effects of Abandonment on the Family

And be careful of [your duty to] God in whose name you demand [your rights] from one another, and [to] the ties of relationship; surely God is ever watchful over you! (The Holy Quran 4:1)

Blessed is the man who walks not in the council of the wicked nor stands in the way of sinners…but his delight is in the law of the Lord, and on His law, he meditates day and night. He is like a tree planted by streams of water that yields its fruit in its season and it's fruit does not wither. (The Holy Bible, Psalm 1:1–4)

In religious communities, maintaining family bonds is part of the basic obligation of a believer. Nevertheless, our history as Muslims and Christians is stained with far too many examples of men abandoning their wives and children despite declaring that they practice and love their religion. They will throw away seemingly good reputations as fathers, sons, husbands, brothers, and professionals and, even worse, tarnish their vows, commitments, and dedication to the religion. These commitments will not deter him from leaving the family psychologically abused and traumatized all while professing to be God-conscious. These commitments will not make him choose the more honorable route of maintaining the marriage vows or, at the very least, a planned separation and/or divorce.

And if you fear a separation between the two of them, appoint an arbitrator from his fam-

ily and an arbitrator from her family... Verily
Allah is Knowing, Knowledgeable. (Quran 4:35)

Of course, everyone makes mistakes. The remedy for that is
repentance. But mistakes and carefully orchestrated manipulation are
not the same, especially if it is habitual. In the Quran and Hadiths,
the word *tawbah* (to return) means to turn away from forbidden acts
and return to Allah. This includes correcting the wrong and ceasing
the forbidden act in the future.

The habitual abandoning narcissist, with his overwhelming
sense of entitlement, will find repentance and mending his ways
almost impossible. He will happily indulge in his mental and physical addictions. From the outside, it may seem that he has gotten away
with such atrocities and is happily living in his reinvented life. But
remember, there is no true happiness or rest for the untreated narcissist. He will spend most of his time working hard at maintaining
and/or repairing the counterfeit persona that he coveted. For a time,
he will appear to be extremely happy, until one day, like with you and
the one before you and the one before her, the mask will slip off and
he must run...again! In fact, he will never be able to stop running
until he repents and mends his ways.

Ask yourself, What kind of life can someone who is constantly
on the run, hiding, and covering lie after lie have? Men who use this
as a way of life lie continuously. They lie about big things, and they
even lie about little things just to test the waters just to see if he can
get away with the lie. One lady I spoke with said her husband would
get new tattoos and if she would mention it, he would say it was not
new. She didn't know why he was lying about it because she also had
a few tattoos and would not have complained about them. It seems
that he would lie for no reason. Can he have any real peace or happiness when he must juggle multiple compartmented lives between
family, friends, work, religious community, home, and his hidden
alternate lifestyle? Making sure they merge just enough to keep up
appearances but not so much as to expose his counterfeit persona?
But the narcissist does want happiness; however, due to the dysfunction that has been left untreated, he will ruin every chance of happi-

ness that he encounters. His attempts will always result in a trail of broken spirits, destroyed families, and generational dysfunction.

Repentance is key to the positive development of the spirit and staying on the path toward Allah. Prophet Muhammad (PBUH) narrated that Allah says, "As soon as My servant makes a step toward me, I make two steps toward him; as soon as he comes to Me walking, I come to him running." The *tawbah* (repentance) should be earnest in heart and free from sanctimony and insincerity.

As noted previously, many experts believe that the abandoning spouse was probably psychologically wounded or abandoned himself in childhood. This has caused him to be unable to develop proper attachments beyond the superficial and/or physical in the relationship. We may ask, How does one reconcile this behavior with being a believer? We must leave Allah to be the final judge of this destructive behavior while we devote ourselves to the protection and healing of women and children devastated by this conduct.

> The just and fair will be seated on chairs of light before Allah, such people are those who decide with justice and deal justly in matters relating to their families and other affairs entrusted to them. (Prophet Muhammad, PBUH)

Abandonment will catastrophically disrupt the family dynamic. During this episode, the family will not have the benefit of preparation as in a planned separation or divorce. The mother will have no way to protect the children from this upheaval.

If he has authority and uses it to harm others—mentally or physically—instead of using his position to protect the family, it shows lack of character and empathy and pure malice. He has authority in the marriage and in the community as Allah has given men the leadership role to protect and maintain women. Our communities have women and children who lack or have shortage of food, clothing, and shelter because of abandonment. This abandonment is a clear example of cruelty and lack of empathy for anyone beyond himself. We know that all deeds, good or bad, are judged by the intent.

Premeditated and orchestrated abandonment shows immoral and cruel intent.

His abrupt severing of the family can cause the same feelings and distress as a sudden death in the family. Those affected go through all the same stages of grief: denial, anger, bargaining, depression, acceptance, and the newly added stage of meaning. This change will cause temporary or long-term anxieties until the wife and children can restabilize emotionally, psychologically, and financially. This could cause temporary or long-term trauma and can become the gateway for generational economic struggle and abuse. Therefore, proper measures such as leaning on and reinforcing faith and God-consciousness in conjunction with family and individual counseling and financial support must be taken.

Case Study No. 4. "We sold our home with the intention of downsizing. We did this because he wanted to change jobs for the second time, taking huge pay cuts with each new position. We ended up purchasing a home that cost us more than the house we had just sold. After being in our new house for just two weeks, he sprung a divorce on me. We had to short sell the house and lost all the equity we had accumulated from our previous house. During our relationship, one of the ways he dealt with his bad moods or insecurities was shopping. When he left, we were upside down in both cars and our house. We had credit card debt, a debt to my parents, and no savings."

Case Study No. 5. "When he abandoned us, I emailed him that day to say that he must adhere to his legal and Islamic financial obligations no matter where he is living or with whom. He said that he would pay the mortgage as was our financial routine but then refused, saying he would only pay one month. It wasn't until I took him to court that I was able to get spousal support. Even then, he tried to file an appeal to end the support, but his appeal was denied. We had numerous financial obligations to two homes, one of which he tried to sell out from under me, and I was also caring for my father as well. Instead of abandoning, he should have just come forward because making a plan for separation would have been easier emotionally and financially, but I quickly learned this was not his goal."

> And when you divorce women and they
> have [nearly] fulfilled their term, either retain
> them according to acceptable terms or release
> them according to acceptable terms, and do
> not keep them, intending harm, to transgress
> [against them]. And whoever does that has certainly wronged himself. (Quran 2:231)

The Children

The sudden absence of the parent, stepparent, or guardian can cause a range of behavior from mild to severe depending on the age of the children and their previous bond with the absent parent. In many cases, this severing of the family also includes the family of the husband. They will also become estranged if they were manipulated to accommodate his actions. Worldwide, one-third of mental health conditions can be traced back to adverse childhood experiences.[18]

Common belief among professionals is that if a parent or caregiver physically abandons young children, they are severely traumatized. Just like adults, they experience a mixture of devastation, shock, confusion, and shame, which can lead to low self-esteem. This may happen even if other adults in the family step in as support systems. This type of pain causes feelings of guilt that they did something to cause this abandonment. If they are very young and can't understand what has happened, they may also have the added fears that the remaining parent may also leave. The children may hope and pray for a reunion as they continue to mourn the loss. If the abandoning parent starts or attaches to a new family while he is reinventing him-

---

[18] Hailey Shafir, "Abandonment Issues: Signs, Causes, and How to Overcome," ed., Benjamin Troy (2020, 2022).

self, this only adds to the feelings of inadequacy for the children as their perception is that they have been "discarded and replaced."

Brad Bushman's study in the National Academy of Sciences was the first to look at the origins of narcissism. His study showed that people are not born narcissists but that it is the way parents treat their children that leads to narcissism. He surmised that while loving your child is healthy, thinking that your child is better than other children can lead to narcissism, and there is nothing healthy about narcissism. "People with high self-esteem think they're as good as others, whereas narcissists think they're better than others. Self-esteem and narcissism also develop in different ways, the study found. While parental overvaluation was associated with higher levels of child narcissism over time, it was not associated with more self-esteem. In contrast, parents who showed more emotional warmth did have children with higher self-esteem over time. Parental warmth was not associated with narcissism."[19]

On the other side of overindulgence is parents who don't allow their child to acknowledge their feelings or grief. This can lead to depression, anxiety, anger, rage, or even lack of empathy for others. All these play a role in a person's inability to truly connect with others, including a spouse. Narcissistic abuse and abandonment can thrive in this type of environment. If a child is a victim of emotional or physical abandonment, there are many possible outcomes for their outlook on relationships going forward. They may decide that this is acceptable and inflict this abandonment on others or become emotionally closed off in relationships. Hopefully, they will decide to seek help to address this childhood trauma head-on to avoid creating a generational system of abuse and dysfunction.

Just as harmful as being raised in a family that does not allow for the acknowledgment of feelings is being raised with the narcissist. Children of the narcissist live in the same cycle of abuse as all others around the narcissist. They are in a never-ending cycle of love-bombing and spirit-breaking and silent treatments. They can possibly stay

---

[19] Ohio State University News, "How Parents May Help to Create Their Own Little Narcissists" (March 9, 2015).

in stage 1 (love-bombing) and stage 2 (spirit-breaking) for the duration of their childhood or until they are abandoned once and for all. Tragically, they can be abandoned multiple times and in multiple ways. If children begin to see and reject the hypocrisy or recognize his cycle of abuse, he will turn on them just as he will turn on anyone else. No one is spared from the narcissist's abusive ways.

Case Study No. 1. "I didn't immediately tell my children, but they could see that I was in distress emotionally. I eventually told them so they could also see how we must continue to work through any hardships that we are having. I tried to shelter them, but they were very much affected by this."

Case Study No. 4. "My daughter was almost four when we divorced. Now at the age of twenty, she is currently coming to grips with her dad's behavior. We shared fifty-fifty custody. As a result, she experienced years of his manipulation. I tried my best to never speak poorly of him to her. Due to his treatment of her, she is currently working on her tendency to be a people pleaser."

Case Study No. 5. "My son was with us when he abandoned us on the vacation. When we arrived home, he was devastated. I tried to console him, but he was understandably inconsolable. He is still working through very extreme anger that he has verbalized is due to this event. It seemed as though they were inseparable, yet he walked away without warning. My son was devastated."

Children, like the wife, are a constant supply for the narcissist. That is because children will give unconditional love and admiration that unknowingly fuel the narcissist. The child that is deprived of attention will began to seek it out from that narcissistic parent. Once the child obtains the affection of the narcissistic parent, the parent will manipulate that child. He will also turn the children against each other by praising one and demeaning the others openly or privately. The manipulative parent will shamelessly complain about one child to the other. The "favorite" may be groomed to be the next generation narcissist, or all the children can be subjugated to stage 1 (love-bombing) and stage 2 (spirit-breaking). Without the capacity of true empathy, the narcissist is incapable of truly loving anyone. Children are even a means to an end for the narcissist, and their life with him is a roller coaster and revolving door of emotions, changing rules, changing personas, and manipulation. He will also use children as bait in stage 1 (love-bombing).

Case Study No. 1. "He wanted to purchase a home for me and described what it would look like in great detail. When I shared with him how deeply hurt I was that my children's father refused to play an active role in their lives, he talked about being a good father figure to my children."

Case Study No. 5. "I was a divorced single mother of a male child. He constantly spoke of how he would love to be a support system for me as well as for my son. This weighed heavily on my decision to marry him. However, when he abandoned us, the last thing I said was, 'Are you going to at least say goodbye to my son [who was with us]?' He kept walking. Later, my son described seeing him rushing around that morning but didn't know why."

The child of the narcissist grows up in a fog of lies, deception, manipulation, love-bombing, indulgence in material things, and pressure to be overachievers because their achievements reflect the narcissist's reputation that he covets. To achieve for their own self-worth is not the goal of the narcissistic parent who pushes perfection. Every road begins with and leads to the gratification of the narcissist.

Everyone around must capitulate and be a pawn in developing and maintaining his counterfeit persona. His children are likely to think that "love-bombing" is real love, and they will begin to seek out love-bombing in friends and future spouses. The children will be constantly, even as adults, ruled by fear, obligations, guilt, rewarding with affection and/or gifts, and punishing with demeaning, spirit-breaking, withholding accolades, raging, and/or silent treatments.

Silent treatments are the narcissist's go-to for the least infraction, and since the rules are always changing, an infraction is always around the corner for the child of a narcissist. Just like the spouse of a narcissist, children are also at risk every moment of being punished or discarded. The child of a narcissist can easily become an adult wracked with anxiety, fear, and/or low self-esteem and are at risk of becoming a people pleaser and drawn in by a narcissistic spouse.

However, that child can also become the narcissist and inflict this cycle on another generation.

The narcissist will even go as far as to alienate the children from the other parent to maintain control. Since the narcissist is the perpetual "shape-shifter" as he goes from wife to wife, he will reinvent himself, which can cause confusion and resistance among the minor or adult children. If they are still seeking approval, they will cover for the parent, but if they have seen behind the mask, they may object to the new rules enforced by the narcissist while he is reinventing his life.

For example, while with one family, drinking, smoking, revealing dress, and other worldly behaviors may be acceptable. However, when the narcissist reinvents himself, all those around will become confused because now the rules have changed and these behaviors are no longer acceptable in the reinvented life. This scenario can be in the reverse. If this contradiction or resistance becomes apparent to the new spouse, he will say that the "defiant children" are yet another example of the many people who do not appreciate him or who keep him from his own success or spiritual growth.

But children raised by or in a home with a narcissist are not doomed. They can grow to be well-adjusted, empathetic adults. This can happen if they recognize or learn about these behaviors and free themselves of trying to appease the dysfunctional parent, they can take corrective action to stop the generational cycle of dysfunction. There are many reputable books and therapists that can assist in this process and aid in the children's recovery from narcissistic manipulation and abuse from a parent.

While writing this book, I spoke to a gentleman who told me about the trauma that his mother suffered that led to a nervous breakdown and hospitalization because of his father's abandonment of the family. The children also suffered as they were tragically taken into foster care during the mother's illness. This grandfather talked about how his mother suffered and how she was never quite the same. Even in his voice at that moment, as a grandfather, I could hear the pain and anguish that he felt for his mother to this day.

The Wife

This type of sudden severing of the family will lead to overwhelming mental, spiritual, and financial stress for the wife. If this abandonment also includes desertion, which is removal of financial support from the home, the wife will not be able to properly care for the children, especially if he was the sole breadwinner. In cases where the wife is also working, it could still create not only financial hardship but also mental and emotional stress, which can lead to problems at work and/or job loss, creating a domino effect. Loss of employment can lead to losing the ability to provide food, clothing, shelter, transportation, and/or health care. Just imagine the countless women and children you have seen on the street. Do you ever wonder *how* some of them came to be in this situation?

The wife was a prop in his manufactured life. She was a means to an end, self-gratification. Although she may ask herself, "Why wasn't I enough?" it is precisely the opposite. He found something in her that he covets and/or envies, and that is why she was chosen. Perhaps, she could promote his image by being what he aspires to be, the power couple. She could have strengthened his weaknesses, such as hidden low self-esteem, by being a constant source of admiration; she could possibly mend the family history of dysfunction by providing stability or a host of other things. He covets reputation, status, prestige, money, and/or physical pleasure. Unfortunately, coveting these things are not ingredients for a healthy, productive marriage based on God-consciousness or even just based on decency. The wife was chosen for her value, not for the diminished worth that he will try to have her believe and leave her with.

Regrettably for the wife, narcissists project all their bad behavior onto the spouse. This is done in two ways: first, by backbiting the spouse, and secondly, by mistreating the spouse privately. This, of course, is in stage 2 (demeaning and spirit-breaking). If he treats everyone, including the spouse, with the best behavior publicly, it will create doubt about her mistreatment privately. This *is* a deliberate process.

Case Study No. 3. "He did not have a problem with showing me off at his masjid. He proudly swung me around the community, showed me off to everybody who was looking. That was a big part of his draw to me. I think he thought I was good arm candy. The very next day, after the wedding, he began demeaning me. The honeymoon was hell."

Case Study No. 5. "When I told two close friends about the abandonment, they were shocked, both recalling to me that the previous weekend he was singing my praises when they saw him at his event that I planned for him. I sadly recalled to them that when we arrived home from that same event, I asked if he felt it was successful. He scowled at me that I had only planned his book signing to bring customers to my store, not for him. I was shocked."

Why was I Selected?

As a wife, the reasons this personality type will seek you out is because of the good qualities that you possess, such as empathy and compassion. Therefore, do not feel the need to change yourself to avoid being a target. Rather than see these qualities as a liability, use the knowledge gained about this process to sharpen your radar and fine-tune your skills in spotting and dealing with the predatory narcissist. Make sure you seek the professional help you need to overcome damage and baggage from previous relationships in childhood or marriage that may cause you to be a target. And of course, first and foremost, rely on your belief in the Creator that all things—even bad things—happen for a reason and that He is the best of planners!

The narcissist seeks out someone who (1) elevates his status, (2) has an open heart, (3) is sensitive to the plight of others/a helper and nurturer, (4) has already been abused in some way by parents or a previous relationship or spouse, and/or (5) if you pass his litmus test, which is, if you catch him in a lie, he can wiggle out of it. He will, in fact, tell a lie or some scandalous secret to see if you will overlook it. These are some of, but not all, the tests that you might have "passed" that allowed you to become a target. For example, fraud experts warn it is common in foreign mail and internet schemes that the con artist will intentionally misspell words in their communications with the target. If the target overlooks this, the predator knows that they can be easily manipulated, but if the target points out the mistakes and becomes suspicious, the con artist will move on to the next potential victim. The predatory narcissist will use this tactic by planting seeds of small lies, inconsistencies, or revealing small unscrupulous secrets of his own to test your pliability.

Case Study No. 2. "He sent messages by his friends for us to meet after I had finally moved on. He was shocked that I would not meet with him. When he would see me at public events, he would send people over to deliver messages. This was nothing new, but I continued to keep my distance, not to be pulled back in. I finally took my life back."

Case Study No. 4. "The manipulation was a slow walk. What I mean by that is, it started with just going to the local porn store and looking at magazines, to which I objected. Then it was getting some movies. The next thing I know, we owned a huge library of pornography."

Case Study No. 5. "While out on a date night, my husband shockingly ordered nonalcoholic beer. When I protested, saying that it does have alcohol in it, he was agitated and asked the waitress to bring a different glass for the beer. I continued to protest, saying we are Muslims and it shouldn't be on the table at all. I finally stopped because I didn't want to ruin our date night. In hindsight, this was one of several tests where I failed to meet his expectations of compliance. I was later told by an ex that he drank alcohol regularly and that she met him with a drink in his hand."

Surprisingly, you can be discarded while he is still in the home. Belittling, mocking, gaslighting, silent treatments, and disappearing acts for hours or days or weeks can all occur before the final discard of the marriage. These acts will sometimes be followed up by rewards for enduring the abuse, like returning with gifts, praise, attention, and acts of intimacy only to start the cycle again. The discard may be subtle in stages over time or all at once in a final disappearing act or ghosting because (1) this is how he derives his control and pleasure and (2) he is likely setting up the next victim and is buying time because the narcissist, like a leech, does not like to be without a host. He will not end the marriage like a healthy, well-adjusted adult; instead, he will toy with the unsuspecting victim.

Case Study No. 5. "While driving home from the state where he abandoned my son and me, I texted him to say that the pet boarding called and she was still there and if he is going to pick her up before closing. I could not figure out why she would be there because he left us in the hotel, saying he was going home. He responded, "Are you asking me or telling me?" I did not respond because I did not want to argue and I was driving eight hours in a storm alone with my son to get home. It was weird that he texted nothing about leaving us in South Carolina. I arrived home just three hours later only to find that he had cleared out all his personal belongings from the home, including passport, deed to our second home, even books from the shelves. It was clear that even during the text while I was driving, he had already moved out."

He will play a host of manipulative games to string you along and to buy time to build a bridge to the next relationship. He will be outwardly overconfident and arrogant. However, he will inwardly seek attention to fuel his ego. In addition, he is consumed with fear of being caught and full of contempt for those who do not have to live a life of deception.

When he finally abandons, as he is a person full of contradictions, you may assume that he is running to live a life of luxury with his new target. However, he is just as likely living in a seedy den of drugs, alcohol, random women, and/or undercover homosexual activity as he is free now to indulge in all the behaviors and addictions that were hidden during the marriage. A vacation of sorts between respectable, image-building targets.

Case Study No. 3. "He was constantly telling me stories of his previous street life as if it were in the past. Because he spoke of that lifestyle in past tense, I treated it like it was also in the past. After the abandonment, I learned that he was still secretly indulging in this life of drugs and other crimes."

Case Study No. 4. "I wish I had asked questions about his mental health. Afterward, I learned that he had been diagnosed with borderline personality disorder."

Case Study No. 5. "Giving me blow by blow of his escapades before becoming Muslim seemed to be a source of pleasure and entertainment for him. The more shocked I was, the more pleased he seemed to be with himself. I would sometimes say, 'You probably should have kept that to yourself.' He didn't start telling me these stories until after marriage, the first time on the morning after our wedding. I would think to myself that he must be making this up to seem like a 'bad boy,' not realizing these things were true."

The untreated narcissist is living a life of misery as the one thing he seeks and covets—true happiness—will forever elude him. He will seem to be "winning" in the short game, getting adulation, attention, and uncommitted physical fulfillment. However, the long-term goal—tranquility in a marriage based on faith, love, and respect—will continue to stay out of his reach. He will spend his life "marriage hopping" until he becomes too old to keep up with the 24/7, 365-days-a-year job of deception, managing multiple lives, and fear of being caught in a hidden lifestyle.

Case Study No. 5. "When my brother-in-law, who is also an Imam/Minister, made an inquiry to the Christian church where my Muslim husband was giving a sermon, he said that he was concerned about the false image of Islam that was presented and any other women becoming a victim of his deception. The response was, 'You do not have to worry about that because everyone here is gay.' Of course, people have the right to practice and believe what they want. However, it was still very shocking to hear this information. When did this become a part of his lifestyle or belief system?"

> It was narrated from Ibn Abbas that the Prophet said: "The best of you is the one who is best to his wife, and I am the best of you to my wives." (Ibn Majah Book 9, Hadith 1977)

Narcissistic abuse has both short- and long-term effects no matter how long or short the marriage. This type of control and manipulation is slow, subtle, and deliberate. Although over time you *will* heal and survive this type of abusive relationship, you can possibly suffer extreme emotional and psychological damage. This damage can affect current and future relationships if you do not seek professional psychological and spiritual guidance. Please know, this, too, shall pass! The Creator has promised us that after every hardship, He will bring us ease, and His promise is always true!

Many victims of abandonment can experience symptoms of PTSD (post-traumatic stress disorder), causing persistent thoughts and flashbacks, anxiety, fear, and depression. All these can cause mental, psychological, even physical illness. The body's reaction to this distress can include headaches, body aches, and eating problems that can lead to weight loss or weight gain.

Case Study No. 1. "I am currently in ongoing therapy. I was questioning my self-worth to the point of thinking, 'Why wasn't I good enough to be selected? Why wasn't I a choice? Was I not pretty enough?' I didn't share too much with my children at the time, but there was some effect on them nonetheless. They saw me shut myself off and needing space and time. Over time, I was honest with them about what I was going through so they could grow and learn for themselves that you can seek help and pick up the pieces. They were aware that I was not well emotionally."

Case Study No. 2. "Although my hair began to thin out from the stress, I never had any other physical illness. I experienced depression. To this day—it has been three years—I still have trauma and anxiety when I think about all that I went through and the deception and manipulation I was subjected to."

Case Study No. 4. "I have had much counseling as well as building my relationship with God. The counseling has given me very practical understanding of the dynamics at play and my part in the dysfunction. Working on my relationship with God has helped me to believe and embody that I am special. I am fearfully and wonderfully made. I deserve to be loved and cherished by my husband."

Case Study No. 5. "My son and I were in counseling immediately. It felt like 'my husband' and his 'stepfather' had died tragically on the vacation. We went through all the stages of grief, compounded by grieving for my father, who lived with us but died six weeks later. There were no condolences from my spouse or his family. My son and I had a Muslim counselor who provides individual and family therapy. I also had a Christian therapist, a woman who was provided through my employer because the stress had begun to affect my productivity. In hindsight, it was good to have both—male and female—counselors when dealing with our trauma."

> Should they intend to deceive thee, verily Allah sufficeth thee: He it is That hath strengthened thee with His aid and with [the company of] the Believers. (Quran 8:62)

> Their malice may be concealed by deception, but their wickedness will be exposed in the assembly. (The Holy Bible, Proverbs 26:26)

After being victimized, you may experience fear of being in public places as your confidence in your ability to determine unsafe situations may have diminished. You may feel overwhelming shame at not being able to detect this level of manipulation, deception, and frankly, danger. The only way to overcome is to speak out, to speak truth to your own power with purpose. There may be people around you who want you to feel shame at being abandoned, and they may advise you to remain silent. Some well-meaning family and friends may advise you to be silent because they do not want you to suffer additional scrutiny or harm. However, others want your silence because they may be complicit. They—and your abuser—want you to be quiet because they want to be comfortable. If you speak out about what you have suffered and about your abuse, these people cannot go on comfortably believing the counterfeit persona that he has presented. Something that looks good, even if it is a lie, is often more comfortable for those watching. They can close their eyes and ears to your trauma so they can sleep at night. Also, you must realize that everyone who celebrated your happiness openly was not always happy for you privately.

If you are a victim of abandonment, you may be questioned by others as to why you painted a good picture of the marriage. However, you may have been just giving a view of the "stage play" that you were experiencing. You may be afraid to come forward, because much like victims of physical or sexual abuse, you do not want to be revictimized by going under the microscope of those who don't want to see him in his true light.

Case Study No. 5. "When I told a close friend about the abandonment, she said, 'Why didn't you tell me that something was wrong?' How could I? For three days, there was a person that I didn't recognize. Day 4, our anniversary, he gave me a card with a handwritten message, 'Alhamdulillah [all praise to God]! Thank you for four wonderful years of marriage.' Two days later, they (the stranger and my husband) were gone. I was told that he had done this Dr. Jekyll–Mr. Hyde routine before."

> The Prophet of Allah also stated: "None would respect women except the magnanimous ones, and none would insult them except the ignoble ones." In addition, the Prophet of Allah stated: "Whoever insults his family, would lose happiness in his life." (Mawa iz al-Adadiyyah)

The Community

> Prophet Muhammad (PBUH) said: "Allah does not punish the individuals for the sins of the community until they see the evil spreading among themselves, and while they have the power to stop it, do not do so." (Ahmad)

This type of abuse threatens the entire community, especially if the person has been put in a position of leadership, authority, or influence. Ideally, the religious community is based on faith, sincerity, and the protection of the rights and needs of every member. The male leaders in the community should be a beacon of support and a guide for education and commitment to family life through their words and deeds. The leader of a religious community should exhibit religious, family, and social responsibility to the highest degree. These traits and qualities should also translate to the husband in this role as the leader and protector of the family and home.

These qualities of protector, maintainer, and educator are what make him suitable to be a community leader and a husband. Of course, these traits and characteristics are relative. His goal should not be to abandon the marriage, but it should be to maintain and grow the family, preserve the marriage, and thus maintain and grow the community. The husband should be a guide for the family to build it up, not to tear it down. His commitment to protect and maintain should be upheld even in times of dissension. Even during the demise of the marriage, he should strive to continue to protect and maintain the family, even if it must be done from a separate location. The shameful act of abandonment *should* be beneath him— spiritually, mentally, and intellectually—as it contradicts the values of his faith and his position as a leader and an intellectual.

One of the most despised characteristics is hypocrisy. The believer should never be a hypocrite; he is clear and transparent in all his dealings. The Prophet said, "One of the worst people is a double-faced man, who comes to one group with one face and to another group with a totally different face" (Al-Bukhari).

Case Study No. 5. "When I saw this video of him in a church giving a Sunday morning talk saying that you must put down organized religion because it does not work and that Salat [Muslims' form of prayer] did not work for him, my mouth was literally hanging open. Was this the new him? The real him or the old him?"

If you are part of a close-knit community—whether Muslim, Christian, Jewish, or otherwise—the acts of abandonment can ripple through the community, affecting men, women, and children. Community life is the cornerstone of all places of worship. There are safeguards in place to build strong families that, in turn, support strong religious and secular communities. When abandonment becomes a practice within a community, it can result in the breakdown of the institution itself, especially if it is so prevalent that it becomes an expectation drawing responses such as "It happens all the time. She should just move on." In addition, it can prevent many communities from growing if there is a perception that this practice will go unchecked by the leaders of the community. Do you know a list of friends who would want to sign up for this type of abuse? Of course not! So it is paramount that this is not tolerated, and perpetrators are exposed—if not even expelled from the community—unless and until they repent and make amends.

> Oh you who believe! Turn to Allah with sincere repentance. (Quran 66:8)

> If we confess our sins, He is faithful and just to forgive us our sins and to cleanse us from all unrighteousness. (Holy Bible, 1 John 1:9)

Of course, forgiveness and repentance (with correction and ceasing the behavior) is the step that needs to be taken after abandonment of the family. However, if someone suffers from narcissistic personality disorder or narcissistic tendencies, this can be exceedingly difficult. In fact, rather than repent, he is more likely to continue this behavior throughout his adulthood until he becomes too old to keep up the charade and/or less desirable because manipulation, as opposed to honesty, requires constant work.

If he and his wife and family are part of a close-knit community, other community members experience at least temporary or maybe even long-lasting stress and distrust from the shift in the safety and security of the community bond. This is especially true if community members entrusted their children to him or sought his advice on spiritual or family issues. The community members would have experienced the same process of manipulation. Their loss, although it may not be as debilitating, is just as real and must be addressed.

The community members or congregation must deal with the very real consequences of the loss of trust in a leader in the community. After they recover from the shock, they must also contend with how this behavior can simultaneously exist with the tenants of the religion, which is a true oxymoron. Instead of coming forward and being transparent and repenting and seeking forgiveness, he is likely, in his true narcissistic way, to become infuriated with the congregation for questioning his actions. He may remind them that they are supposed to practice forgiveness, although he is not offering an apology or explanation. The ever-cunning narcissist may ask them to remember all his well-placed acts of kindness while sowing discord and disruption, turning them against the victim and/or each other. On the other hand, he may dismiss the entire congregation, citing all the ways that they are beneath him, which, in his world, releases him of any responsibility to the people who viewed him as a leader or authority figure. These are the actions of a person who lacks empathy, respect, or concern as most narcissists do, not the actions of a well-adjusted man who has made a mistake for which he is willing to take responsibility and to seek repentance and mend his ways.

In extreme cases, he can further compromise the stability of the community if he was also entrusted with property and/or finances that might have been squandered during this process. This type of ongoing abuse can cause significant damage not only to the community but also to the perception of the religion in general. For example, you may find the reinvented narcissist emerge with new language, like "I subscribe to spirituality," "I don't follow organized religion," or "I left that church/mosque or sect of the religion," citing some flaw or shortcoming of the community or the religion. To avoid accountability, he might claim he has been ostracized or blackballed and seek refuge and reinvention in another community or religion altogether. In his mind, this will absolve him of any responsibility to the tenants of the religion that he proclaimed not only to follow but also where he used to lead and/or advise others. That is because he will subscribe to whomever will give him accolades, admiration, or a stage on which to perform. He will subscribe to the next best opportunity to deceive, manipulate, and/or abuse any congregation, which is only done by a true hypocrite. Because he is a hypocrite and an opportunistic shape-shifter, he will conform to whatever religious beliefs or lifestyle that the current target believes in, and he will put on a Broadway-caliber performance. Religion is a major gateway, and he will not stop using this to manipulate his target.

> And Allah will surely ascertain who are the believers and who are the hypocrites. (Quran 29:11)

Manipulation and deception can rise to the level of oppression for the individual, the family, and the community. According to *The Psychology of Oppression* by Dr. E. J. R. David and Dr. Annie Derthick, oppression can exist subtly and/or blatantly. They go on to say that oppression can be interpersonal, institutional, and internal. "The three levels of oppression are linked with each other and all three feed off and reinforce each other. In other words, all three levels of oppression work together to maintain a state of oppression."[20] Dismissing an individual's (or community's) importance, name-calling, withholding respect and/or affection, and diminishing self-worth are some, but not all, forms of oppression.

Abandonment and the lack of acknowledgment from the authorities in the community rise to the level of oppression. If religious communities want to truly fight the oppression of women, they must appoint a body of people that are also representative of women and entrust them with the authority to hear and make decisions about complaints lodged to the leadership. That body must be free of conflict of interest and have a standard operating procedure for dealing with any and all complaints and be willing to apply enforcement action equally.

Immediately reporting the abuse can still result in leaders turning a blind eye to the misconduct. This can happen if the leaders are incompetent, historically avoid issues of conflict, are in fear of losing their position, or if they themselves are guilty of these behaviors and

---

[20] E. J. R. David and Annie Derthick, *The Psychology of Oppression* (2017).

fear exposure. More honorable leaders may act immediately as they understand their role is not only to lead when things are going well but also to lead in times of disruption. In some communities, the perpetrators of severe misconduct are disciplined by removing them from the positions of authority and/or restricting their participation in some aspects of community life. Although this may seem harsh, it is sometimes necessary to restore a sense of justice, security, and integrity in the community. The harshest discipline should be reserved for gross misconduct that is intentional and/or results in unethical, harmful, or dangerous behavior. Abandonment does rise to this level of gross misconduct as it is unethical and intentional harm, especially when other remedies given in the Quran, Bible, and other scriptures were not used, and instead, he chose to inflict psychological and emotional trauma on the wife, children, and community.

As believing people, we are to forgive sins, including oppression, but we are also instructed to fight oppression wherever we should find it and to continue fighting it until the offender ceases this behavior. It must be dealt with head-on so the behavior does not become normalized and acceptable in the community. This will do irreparable damage to the integrity and growth of the community and will also fuel resentment among those who were not protected when they requested help or support. In addition, witnesses to the inaction will fear coming forward themselves if they are abused, oppressed, or otherwise injured. While conducting research to write this book, I spoke with individuals from various communities who had experienced this type of deception. These members expressed their fear of coming forward if they should experience abuse because they thought they might be blamed or not get support. Also, a woman expressed her ongoing distress and struggle with coming to terms with how someone with whom she entrusted her children and their own spiritual guidance would behave in such a despicable way against his wife and children.

CHAPTER 6

Beware of the Nine Red Flags during Courtship!

There are two routes to red flags in courtship. The first is the man who is reluctant to formally commit and tries to have a causal relationship. He doesn't want to go through a wali/wakil, minister, trusted adviser, or family member; doesn't have strong ties to the religious community; and dismisses the process.

This is not the method of procedure for the habitual abandoning narcissist. He *will* be 100 percent ready for marriage on day *1*! He will happily answer all inquiries; meet with the minister, Imam, wali, or parents and/or family; and present as a highly eligible prospect. He will lead with his ability to charm and gain trust and will be armed with "You *know* me." This "knowledge" of him that he will point out to you will be of his position, title, and/or wealth or maybe charity to the community. It will not be about his practice of the religion, his lifestyle away from the community, or history with treatment of women.

He will direct you to look at superficial qualities because dealing with the narcissist is like accidentally looking into the sun or a bright, shining light, and then for a time, your vision will become blurred and distorted. It's during that period of distortion that he will quickly work his manipulation, aka stage 1 (love-bombing). He will be quick and methodical because even *he* knows that once your vision and senses have returned, he will be gone, aka stage 3 (abandonment/discard)!

So how can you determine if this tranquil life he is presenting is based on an agenda that is less than honorable? It can be quite difficult if you are not adamant because he will use religion and a counterfeit persona as a shield and to hide in plain sight as he works plans of manipulation whose beginning and end is deception and/or abandonment. You must have a litmus test! Measure whatever he is saying, asking, requesting, suggesting by your scriptures. If this measurement comes up short, save yourself and move on! Do this with your head and not your heart, if you have not already been taken in by the highly deceptive narcissist.

Next, let's establish the difference between dating and courtship. Simply put, dating is for getting to know the person, "seeing where things go." Dating, on the surface, has no set purpose other than socializing, pleasure, and/or entertainment. Dating *can* lead to marriage, but that is not the initial intent. There is no formal goal set, and with dating, there may be a physical relationship.

Conversely, courtship is formally stating that marriage is the intended outcome. The courtship period is used to "investigate" the religious, emotional, financial, and social/familial compatibility to establish family life. This process will have a time limit and milestones. The courtship will not include a physical relationship. That is because developing an intimate relationship is not permitted, and premature physical ties will cloud one's judgment in this process. As we know, in religious communities, short courtships are very common and often preferred. Although this is beneficial to keeping the courtship permissible, it can be a place for manipulation by the predator. The courtship should be taken seriously with *Istakara* prayer (prayer to seek counsel), careful investigation, and family and/or community inquiry. These should be done in order to establish his reputation and longevity in the community.

Unfortunately, with his skills of manipulation, you may enter a courtship and regrettably find yourself in a "dateship." The courtship may sound old-fashioned and may seem intrusive, but it is best. Courtship involves getting to know each other in an emotionally, physically, and spiritually safe environment. The wali, Imam, minister, or trusted adviser constantly checks the goals and objectives to ensure the growth and development of the couple *or* to help them determine if they should go their separate ways. One should also consider children as well as parents or other family members who depend on you for their care when making this type of decision!

Please note that not all walis or ministers that provide premarital advice are created equal. Careful selection of your adviser is also required to ensure that he does not have any conflicts of interest with you or the intended fiancé. You want to make sure that the adviser is well established in the community and that you can obtain a good reference for his work as an adviser. This is not required, but of course, doing all you can to protect your own interests is advisable.

You will see that in one of the case studies, the adviser was in a position to prevent the abuse; however, for multiple reasons, he did not or could not. This was due to inexperience and/or bias. He had been compromised and love-bombed as well. Even after she reported that she learned of his past abusive behavior, the adviser admonished her for gossiping instead of looking into the matter. That's because he, too, had been "looking into the sun" or rather the medical degree of the predator, and his vision was distorted. This distortion blinded him from his duty to advise and protect.

The scriptures have made clear the protocol for courtship. Unfortunately, many red flags are often ignored because the proverbial cart has been placed before the horse with premarital counseling coming too late in the process.

While in a roundtable discussion with Naa'ila and Hasan Clay of GLI Counseling Services, they shared with the group that you should seek premarital counseling *before* there is an actual courtship. This will allow you to learn about your must-haves and deal breakers and establish your boundaries. Having premarital counseling before you enter into courtship will also help you learn about red flags through clear eyes and not through the lenses of love-bombing. Attending premarital counseling after the courtship is established is counterproductive to the process established for your protection and even more so if it occurs after the nikah/wedding date has been set. This is because being engaged or setting wedding dates may be seen as points of no return. You may feel pressured to move forward, and he will do just that, as his goal is to be quick to the altar—while you are still looking into the sun—before you see behind the mask of deception that he is wearing.

Another place where the cart can get before the horse is in regulation of ourselves and/or overestimating our ability to appease the narcissist. You might think that getting married will resolve some of his issues of mistrust and/or his need for constant attention or affection. Unfortunately, if his issues are not resolved *before* the marriage, it will inevitably be his reason to abandon the marriage. That is because even during the marriage, you cannot be a constant source of physical affection, adoration, and attention as there are also other members of the household that need attention and other work that needs to be done. Consequently, the untreated narcissist will always find gaps or holes or lack of fulfillment in any marriage to justify abandonment. Therefore, he will continue to marriage-hop because he is not dealing with his issues. He is just shifting the blame and pushing his issues under the rug with each new marriage.

> Shaddad ibn Aws reported: The Prophet, peace and blessings be upon him, said, "The wise man is one who holds himself accountable and performs good deeds to prepare for what comes after death. The foolish man is one who gives into his lowly desires and seeks their indulgence..."
> (Sunan al-Tirmidhī 2459)

There are many red flags that point to the fact that you are dealing with a covert narcissist. The first and most obvious is that he will say that he likes or dislikes or wants whatever you say you like/dislike or want and others. This is called mirroring you during the love-bombing stage. He will do this to create a counterfeit premature bond and to create the illusion that he is your soul mate. For example, he may say that he wants to open a business that you are interested in having or that he also wants to start a family, live/travel abroad, that he is working toward eliminating all his debt, purchasing a home, or creating a college fund for his children. He may say that pilgrimage is his primary goal or going to the masjid or church for payer daily or establishing a religious school. Really, it can be anything big or small that you want to do; he will chime in and say it is his dream as well. In the reverse, he will also dislike anything that you dislike and so on.

During these conversations, you may jump to the conclusion that you have identical wants and needs, so therefore, you must be soul mates, and he will be more than happy to let you jump to that conclusion! However, you *must* follow up with questions. What inspired you to want this (fill in the blank)? What have you done so far toward your debt reduction? What do your family and friends think about the business idea? While with his family, mention his desire to go to the masjid daily for prayer, start this business, grow a family, go on pilgrimage, purchase that home, etc. Gauge their reaction. Do they say "Yes! He has always dreamed of this!" or do they seem surprised or apprehensive and looking around, not knowing what to say? This seems like a lot of work, but so is getting married only to find out none of his aspirations align with yours, and this leads to bigger problems in the marriage. Do your homework on the front end to avoid deception and divorce on the back end. Of course, one's goals can change, but there is still evidence of working toward that goal before it is reassessed.

Narcissists will tell many lies to look more powerful, more appealing, or to seem overly confident. He will be somewhat of a bragger and grandiose. The white-knight narcissist will brag and appear to be humble all at the same time; it is a very neat trick. He will also solicit others (even you) to unknowingly do his bragging for him so he can appear to be humble. He will constantly toot his own horn and say that he doesn't want to toot his own horn over and over, and around and around we go! The very high-functioning manipulator will eventually get you to do all his horn-tooting for him while he relaxes and reaps the rewards. Unfortunately, you may not realize these are lies and the setting for a very elaborate stage play until you are well into stage 2 (demeaning and spirit-breaking) or in stage 3 (abandonment and discard).

Case Study No. 1. "I thought he was the perfect man because he wanted to support and extend my dreams beyond what I had imagined and shared with him. When I told him I was a certified fitness trainer, he quickly responded that he was already working out the details in his head about how he would help me establish a business."

Case Study No. 2. "I found that he was mimicking my thoughts, hopes, and dreams after I shared certain things with him. I also discovered that bonds were beginning to exist when it was just a little too soon in the relationship. In the first few months, he confessed his love for me. After that, he rarely told me he loved me."

Case Study No. 3. "He studied me. Once he found out I had a podcast, he watched every single podcast. The level of study my ex utilized in love-bombing me was exceptional. He watched every podcast multiple times. In retrospect, I now know that he was mirroring me. At the time, I was not consciously aware of this. He raised issues and was passionate about the things I had going on my podcast. He did these things very early on in our attachment, like in the first one to two weeks. He made really huge, grand gestures."

Case Study No. 5. "I told him that I was career-oriented, and this might be a problem for some Muslim men who might prefer a stay-at-home wife and maybe I would not be the best choice for him. He immediately said he was excited about that because we could be a 'power couple' and his previous wives lacked ambition. I told him I had no interest in being a 'power couple.' I later learned that this was not true because his previous wives had successful careers as well."

He will boast about outlandish conversations with supervisors on the job or people that he meets, and you will find yourself thinking, *Who says that and gets away with it?* Or you will find him boasting of belittling people at work or in his personal life. You may find him to be extremely critical of family and friends. His own children, siblings, and even his mother and father will not be safe from his criticisms and disdain. However, he will shower them with affection in their presence. This love-bombing of them will be like, once again, looking into the sun and distorting your vision and wiping away the memory of his harsh verbal criticisms of them when the two of you are alone.

He will see everyone as being beneath him and will gloat at other's misfortune; he will diminish their dreams and laugh openly when you are alone, showing lack of empathy for the struggles of others. Although it seems that these are glaring character flaws, through the lenses of the love-bombing stage, these can easily be missed. That is because they will be separate occurrences, few and far between, and covered in a fog of love, affection, gifting, and charitable acts in between the acts of diminishing you and others.

> And of the people is he whose speech pleases you in worldly life, and he calls Allah to witness as to what is in his heart, yet he is the fiercest of opponents. (Quran 2:204)

> The Lord detests lying lips, but he delights in people who are trustworthy. (The Holy Bible, Proverbs 12:22)

The most obvious problems are easy to spot, like grand plans and boasting and anger at being corrected…ever. Not having empathy for others is a hard one because some narcissists are very good at imitating empathy. Don't get too focused on the obvious signs and miss the small slip-ups that allow the covert narcissist to quietly sneak into your life and leave like an F-5 tornado, destroying everything in his path.

In addition, you must set boundaries and have clear expectations going into courtship. This will be a level of protection from the narcissist. "Relationships have two types of principles. Foundational and negotiable. Foundational values are unwavering. These include matters such as culture, religion, commitment, being debt-free or structured eating habits. Other matters are up for discussion and negotiation. What are your negotiables?"[21] Here are a few, but not all, red flags to beware of what may appear in stage 1 (love-bombing).

Red Flag No. 1
He insists he is ready for marriage immediately!

As flattering as this may be, being immediately ready for marriage is a huge problem:

1. Men who use abandonment as a weapon like to marry quickly, and they leave just as quickly. He will be adamant about a short courtship and use reasons such as the religion or just not being able to wait to make you his wife. That is because he will still be glorifying you at this time. He will never consider that the two of you may not be a good match for each other because you are the current target and because he is only considering the upside for himself. He will rush you and your family to marriage with over-the-top love confessions and accolades to gain your trust. He knows that as a woman, you are prone to thinking with your heart, and he will use this admirable trait to manipulate you.

2. You must be clear on what he is looking for in a spouse. If soul mate, power couple, or any image-/ego-boosting, status-building attributes show up, this is also a problem. This shows that he is more focused on optics for himself rather than building a marriage. He is more focused on obtaining a wife than *being* a husband. He will be a husband as long as it suits him and his persona, and then he will discard the

---

[21] Hasan Clay and Naa'ila Clay, *Selection Perfection* (2021).

marriage when he decides that you are no longer a supply for his immediate wants and needs.

3. What happens if in the courtship he finds out that although you may be what he is looking for that unfortunately he is not going to be the best option for you? An honorable man, upon this realization, may say, "Unfortunately, I cannot provide the [blank] that you require. Therefore, I must bow out." Is the self-serving narcissist going to admit that he cannot fulfill your expectations? Of course not. In fact, he will counter and double down by offering you the sun and the moon because his agenda has nothing to do with putting you in a better position spiritually, emotionally, or financially. This is part of the grooming process not just for you but also for your family and anyone in your circle of protection. You will all be love-bombed while you are in the grooming stage.

Red Flag No. 2
You are giving more information than you are gathering.

He will be overly inquisitive, asking sometimes intruding questions, to appear genuinely attentive. However, this information can be used to manipulate you and your family. *You* should be gathering information. Women like to express themselves, so you will have to control this urge. Remember, you are on a fact-finding mission that can change the course of your life! You may need to do a background check, especially if you have children. A background check is surprisingly inexpensive, and the cost far outweighs the risks of not doing one. The background check can uncover gaps in employment, overlapping marriages, or multiple residences, as well as any legal or financial issues that may affect the marriage and/or your financial standing. This background check can be legal, financial, or by way of mutual acquaintances or community leaders. However, keep in mind that his manipulation can be far-reaching and distort the view of those around you.

Case Study No. 1. "I was also informed by one of his former wives and a prominent wakil in the community that he was married too many times to count. The marriages always ended badly. Many of the marriages lasted less than a year. Had I known this, I may not have given him the time of day. Too many marriages are an indication that an individual may have quite a lot of baggage and some reform to do on himself."

Case Study No. 4. "Ask about any mental diagnosis. I found out long after the divorce that my ex was diagnosed with borderline personality disorder when he was sixteen. It might be an awkward question or discussion. However, if I had known, I hope I would have made a different decision."

Case Study No. 5. "After the abandonment, I began my background check and inquiries. So many things did not add up. In fact, had I done it on the front end and asked him the necessary follow-up questions about these issues, I am confident he would have likely moved on to target someone else. If I had just one five-minute conversation with one of his previous wives, I would have quickly moved on myself."

The narcissist is a shape-shifter, and in essence, he hides everything while appearing to be transparent. He will hide current relationships, as they are known for overlapping relationships and marriages. He will hide his plans of isolating you from family and friends. He will hide his friends as well, and you're not likely to meet or spend any significant time with them, if he has any. He will always have one foot in and one foot out of the marriage. That is because he is always on the lookout for a new target and ready to enter stage 1 (love-bombing) with the next victim. He will also hide his emotions because the narcissist is truly insecure and a very envious and jealous person. He will hide jobs or seeking new employment or getting fired. Even a new job that should be cause for celebration will be hidden until the last minute just for the satisfaction of having some control over the situation and over you. He will delight in always keeping you in the dark and wondering what will happen next. His abrupt departure from and taking new jobs without telling you is a big red flag that he lacks true stability and/or is always full of deception. He will try to hide money, plans, and most of all, his disdain for you and for his other family members, but if you listen carefully, you will hear the blame game constantly in the background like white noise. "If not for [mother, children, ex-wife, brother, father, supervisor, coworker]…I could have done so much more…"

Even his emotions and facial expressions will be manufactured. If you pay attention, you will also see that he is an expert of being "emotionless," a stone wall. He will attempt to hide everything mentally, physically, spiritually, and financially. Amid all this deception, he will show some signs of kindness in front of others to keep you all on the hook. He will do this also to appease the flying monkeys. This will aid him when he does strike; he will lean on these acts of kindness to say he is not what/who you say he is all while running a smear campaign. He will say to them, "*You know me!* You can't believe what your ears are hearing or what your eyes are seeing! You know me!" He will be enraged at and dismissive of anyone who objects or shows you sympathy. That is because behind his anger is fear! The narcissist is afraid of everything. You would be, too, if your entire life was counterfeit and manufactured just to look like a morally upstanding member of the community, to write the narrative of superficial success, yet there are huge gaps in ethical behavior.

Red Flag No. 3
He rejects having the meeting to establish courtship.

I was listening to an online lecture from the Rawdah Islamic Center in Delaware, the Imam/Minister said never come to the meeting to establish courtship alone. Of course, you are very capable of managing your own business. But if you lack support or representation in the sit-down for courtship, it will signal to him that he has already gained your unconditional trust. This will also be a signal that he can isolate you in the courtship or marriage or that he will not have to explain his actions to anyone but you, who may already be viewing him through love-bombed, rose-colored lenses. He may say, "We are grown people. We don't need this!"

He went on to say, ask for a male family member to attend to counter his ego—this pertains to any religion, of course. If you have no male relatives available, bring your aunt/uncle, a sibling, or even a best friend, if all else fails. Someone from your life needs to be a part of this process. They will see/hear things you do not see/hear. You *must* be willing to listen if they object in any way. Remember, *you* brought them because you trust them, so listen to them if they have doubts about him!

Red Flag No. 4
He always says the right thing and tries a bit too hard.

He will say all the right things because he is well rehearsed. A perfect first meeting is a red flag. When something seems too good to be true, it's because it typically is! He will be able to present as a perfect match for you, because as mentioned, he will mimic you. The most genuine people have flaws that are readily seen as they are not hiding their true selves and have a mediocre or less-than-grand first impression. The red flag for the manipulator is, his first impression will "amaze" you and everyone around you. He will be perfect in every way because he is not presenting and will never present his true self until you are in stage 2 (demeaning and spirit-breaking) or stage 3 (abandonment and discard). It is only at this moment of the discard that you will really see the vicious, horrifying person that lives behind the mask.

Red Flag No. 5
He blames his ex-wife/wives for the entire demise.

Multiple marriages and/or having been previously married within one to two years of your courtship is a red flag that is cause for investigation. If he is divorced and exhibits any of the red flags, you should ask to see divorce papers. Ask yourself *and him* what time he spent on self-reflection and actively working to change patterns and/or behaviors to prevent repeating any issues from the previous marriage. Will he drag unfinished issues from that marriage to yours? Did he leave that marriage abruptly after committing some mental or physical abuse, or is he running from or hiding something? How did he dissolve the marriage? Was he responsible and caring, or did he simply abandon the marriage? It is important for you to confidently determine the cause of the divorce(s). Placing all the blame on the previous wife and accepting little or no accountability is a huge red flag.

More likely than not, his family will cover for him because they have seen or been a victim of his manipulation, have always protected him, or just want to avoid family embarrassment or conflict with him. Let's face it. Everyone has problems and makes mistakes. However, if he is unwilling to discuss those mistakes and show how they will not be repeated in your marriage to him, that is an indicator that you will be subjected to this type of blame or abuse as well.

If the reasons for divorce do not add up, you need to fact-check. He may give different reasons based on who's asking. He will use what will be an acceptable reason to each person. You need to ask multiple people and compare notes about the cause of his divorce(s). In some cases, you may even need to fact-check with the ex-wife. If it did not work out after meaningful attempts to repair the marriage but he still treated her with dignity and respect and took care of his responsibilities, then this is considered leaving in good standing, as far as divorce goes. If they have minor children, he should not mind a brief conversation with the ex-wife because the children will, at some point, be in your home and preferably on a regular basis. This can be necessary if for no other reason than to determine expectations on exchanging the children or routines at their mother's home that may need to be kept in your home and how discipline should be handled. If he objects, you should reconsider courtship, or if he ends the courtship because you have asked to speak with her, then you have surely dodged a bullet. If you do your homework, you will likely find multiple reasons for the demise of the marriage that don't add up, but unfortunately, this information may not be revealed until far too late.

Case Study No. 1. "He said he was a good husband to his ex-wife and had even paid for her schooling after they divorced so he could make sure she could take care of the children. He ghosted me the day before we were to sit down to talk with my mother about the marriage. Sometime after that, I was able to speak with his ex-wife about some of the things I heard and had shared with my wali. She said she left the marriage because she was tired of the year of abuse—mental and physical—that she had suffered at his hands. She said the abuse that she suffered was on every level. I found out he had been married and/or engaged so many times that people lost count. He also lied about paying for her education, and although he had a PhD, he did not take care of them financially."

Case Study No. 2. "He always shared with me what they, his ex-wives, did wrong but never said what role he played in the ending of the marriages. It was apparent that he could be difficult, but he could also charm you back into the cycle. I learned that he was a narcissist and definitely controlling."

Case Study No. 3. "There was a huge issue and some sort of drama going on in his life. Come to find out the ex was the one he was still sleeping with and had an ongoing relationship with. He was also still involved in what was supposed to be his past criminal lifestyle. I couldn't figure out why his ex-wife seemed to be losing her mind. She seemed very unstable. He made her sound like she was crazy and just a deranged woman and everything was her fault. But it became very apparent that she was just another victim of narcissistic abuse."

Case Study No. 5. "Afterward, people asked me why I had agreed to be wife number 4. He always had an answer for everything. But all those explanations quickly fell apart. The day after our wedding, he told me about his extreme drug abuse during the first marriage. After my abandonment, I learned that he told my brother-in-law that he ended one of the marriages because she was a heavy drinker, which he never once said to me. I was told that in marriage no. 3, he actually came home one day, said he wanted a divorce, and told her to move out, and soon after this, she found my engagement ring! After all those inconsistent stories, I decided to do my homework to see what else he was lying about."

Red Flag No. 6
Negative Comments about Family

It seems unbelievable, but if you listen carefully, you may hear negative feelings, put-downs, or derogatory comments about family members. On the surface, it can seem like harmless venting of the past, but these comments actually speak volumes about his true feelings about his family.

"My brother is the family disappointment, but I love him anyway." Or blaming family members for being obstacles to his success, "If not for my mother/ex-wife/children, I would have accomplished more." Or "I was always the breadwinner and had to carry the load for everyone because they can never get it together." Or "Don't get too close to my mother, sister, brother, or children, because they are always creating drama."

For him, no one is off-limits for negative comments and opportunities to play the victim: not ex-wives, parents, siblings, not even children. Nor will you be spared! He may discourage you from getting to know or spending time with the family. He will say that this is to *protect you* from their drama. Your invitations and gifts sent to them might not be delivered.

Case Study No. 1. "During the engagement, I sent specially prepared meals to his family's home, but they did not receive them. Or he did not tell them that they were from me."

Case Study No. 3. "There were definitely negative comments about his family. He was always the victim, he was the abused child, he was the abandoned kid. Nobody ever loved him. Nobody gave him anything. That was always his story."

Case Study No. 4. "The way he treated his mother, he said he loved her, but he did not respect her. His joking with her was mean. He complained about her behind her back and used her."

Case Study No. 5. "He would make derogatory comments about his family. At times, I felt embarrassed that he was sharing such personal information about them with me, even as his wife. I chastised him on more than one occasion about the nasty things he would say. In hindsight, he would also tell me not to get too close so I could avoid getting the same mistreatment of previous wives. Even then, I would protest that I didn't think they would mistreat me."

Red Flag No. 7
He does not invite you to his place of worship.

If the two of you are from different communities or religions, it is a good idea to visit his place of worship. This will be a way to determine his involvement in the mosque or church or if he has had gaps that are unexplained. Some information will still escape you. A habit of disappearing from the religious community or "masjid or church hopping" is a big red flag. Ask yourself, Was he in another religious community or just off living an alternate life? Please verify this information! Employers do not allow gaps in a résumé! So how can you overlook gaps in his connection to the religious community, family, or friends? Make him close the gaps in his religious/community/family/marriage résumé!

This will also be a way to inquire about his eligibility for marriage. One of the case studies involves a woman who didn't know, until after her abandonment, that her husband had abandoned his previous wife while she—the current wife—was in courtship with him, aka stage 1 (love-bombing). A visit to his community still may not uncover this information; however, you must trust but verify from every angle. This is your life at stake as well as your children or anyone under your care.

My Christian sisters, if he does not invite you to the religion or at least introduce you to the Muslim community, this is a huge red flag. This will be his method of keeping his two lives separate or even presenting himself as single in the Muslim community, keeping you a secret. He can use this tactic to alienate you from the community, and you will have no support during the discard. The masjid is open to all people, and you do not have to be a Muslim to go to the masjid for any religious or social events and activities. If he does not make this available to you, it is a huge red flag!

Red Flag No. 8
He violates boundaries.

The narcissist does not see you for the person that you are. He only sees you for what he can gain mentally, physically, spiritually, socially, and/or financially. Therefore, he feels entitled to you. You are an extension, possession, or object used to fulfill his needs for mental or physical gratification and image-building. Therefore, he may also be overbearing with your time and violate emotional or physical boundaries. Violating your spoken and even unspoken boundaries is a big red flag. Be careful of "innocent" suggestions to do things that are not the protocol at this stage. He may hint at or make suggestions of haram (impermissible) or questionable things to see if you will go along. He may make himself intrusively available to help you in your home or personal life. This will be so he can hopefully create a crack into which he can slip into and intrude upon your private space or personal business. For example, perhaps you are looking to purchase a home, a new car, or negotiating new employment, and he may offer his assistance. Unfortunately, this will give him access to information that he should not have at this time. This will give him information about your finances or about how much you will be making on that new job. This may seem innocent enough, but this is not the time that he should have access to this information. Although he is vying for the position, he is not yet your husband. Even if there is an official engagement, this is not marriage.

Even after you have established your boundaries, the highly skilled narcissist will still try to manipulate you into sex, drugs, alcohol if he is secretly indulging in this life and thinks he can lure you into it with him. If he thinks he can go undetected by those around you, he will try a host of things to get or keep you off guard. You will find similar scenarios in the case studies presented in the appendices.

Case Study No. 4. "He would constantly look at other women, which gave me low self-esteem, and I was beginning to feel insecure. He suggested we go to a sex shop to spice up the marriage, but I was not at all interested. Once I finally gave in to his pressure, he slow-walked me over the course of nine years into pornography and other activities for his own pleasure. He always said I could say no, but each time I did, it was ignored."

The engagement may be yet another manipulation tactic that may not actually result in marriage. It can also be used as a ploy to get you to lower your guard. He may suggest that since you are officially engaged that some of these protections can be relaxed. This is also found in two of the case studies. If you have seen any of the red flags, remember that this person may be hiding behind the persona of a man who is looking to build a marriage and community life. Don't get manipulated into compromising yourself after the engagement. Stay alert.

Case Study No. 1. "He was a gentleman up until the night he asked me to marry him. My wakil was in another room. After my intended used the bathroom, he came from behind and playfully tickled me, then rubbed his left shoulder against my right shoulder. He was well aware that no physical contact is allowed between a man and a woman unless they are married. I was surprised by what he did but did not object because it was very brief and unexpected. Additionally, I was attracted to him and wanted to be married to him. That played a factor in me not correcting his behavior."

Case Study No. 3. "He completely violated every single boundary I had established, all of them. I had a lot of boundaries, especially when it came to his interaction with other women, my privacy, and even just physical boundaries. He violated each and every one of them all the time. He had a huge issue with boundaries."

Case Study No. 4. "He was overbearing from the beginning and did not allow me to have an opinion or make my own choices. When we first started dating, my parents were going to purchase a car for me as a gift for graduating from college. Instead of getting the car I wanted, he pushed me to get the car he wanted…even down to the color."

Case Study No. 5. "He always pushed all boundaries. Before we officially met, we both attended a site visit of a potential new masjid facility. He was constantly walking or standing closely behind me. Since at times the spaces we were viewing were small, like hallways etc., I would step aside, and I dismissed it because I didn't know him personally at that time and didn't make assumptions. After we were married, I mentioned this to him. He said, 'Yes, I was doing it on purpose.'"

Red Flag No. 9
He does not want a written marriage contract or legal marriage license.

The marriage contract is itself the nikah/marriage and is a requirement under Islamic law, but sadly, many sisters skip this step. Christian and other non-Muslim sisters, you can enact a prenuptial agreement to offer some of the same protections. The state marriage license will *not* ensure all your rights required by Quran and Sunnah. You should have both. If you opt for just a marriage contract or pre-nup, it can still be a good source of protection if it meets the state's requirements of a legal contract and has the appropriate witness signatures. But again, you must check the laws of your state.

The Islamic marriage contract must include four parts to be official: (1) mutual consent; (2) *mahr*/dowry; (3) witnesses; and (4) you should also add some additional details that can include, but may not be limited to, distribution of property, if you will work outside of the home, how you will manage joint or separate finances, housing and maintenance, and of course, spousal support in case of separation or divorce. For Christians, think of some of the things you may put in a prenuptial agreement when thinking in terms of the marriage contract. These are some, but not all, examples of things that can go into the marriage contract. You can find a sample of a marriage contract and a prenuptial agreement in the appendices.

You must also make sure that the marriage contract meets the legal requirements of *your state* to hold up in a court. The requirement may include being notarized and/or legally filed in some way with the court, but please check your state. This contract—if not iron-clad—will be a loophole that he will use to avoid paying the required maintenance/spousal support that is the right of Muslim women and believing women married to Muslim men. If the contract doesn't have the force of law behind it, it will be useless. You would think that honoring his religious obligations would be enough, but a hypocrite will not honor his religious obligations. You are probably thinking, *But he loves me and is upstanding...* That is the stage 1 (love-bombing), and during stage 3 (discard), you will find a totally different person. However, if he is honorable, you will never find yourself in court even if the marriage is dissolved. *Note: If you are a non-Muslim woman marrying a Muslim, you have the same rights as a Muslim woman to negotiate your marriage contract, as well as dowry and the required spousal support!*

If it comes down to a divorce, sometimes religious beliefs on divorce can interfere with an adviser providing the best guidance and/or protection. This can happen in any religion. In this example given by Dr. McBride, the abuse is overlooked by the priest in order to save the marriage. "She told the priest that Ted was abusive, and the priest asked Ted if that was so. Ted did not deny it, but he blamed it on Marion, saying that she just made him so upset. After this emotionally draining session, the priest went to Marion's father to discuss what was best for the couple. Thankfully, Marion saw through the complicity of these men and freed herself from her abusive marriage."[22]

The basic principle about the conditions of the contract is that they are permissible and agreed upon, and if both are met—with the required signatures—the contract must be fulfilled. Prophet Muhammad, blessings and peace of Allah be upon Him, said, "The condition which most deserves to be fulfilled is that by means of which intimacy becomes permissible for you" (narrated by al-Bukhari

---

[22] McBride, *Will I Ever Be Free of You?*

2721 and Muslim 1418). This is referring to the marriage contract. If you did not have a marriage contract or prenuptial agreement, you can also do this postnuptial.

Nevertheless, the basic rule of thumb on the contract's conditions is that they are permissible and valid, whether it's a contract for marriage, prenuptial agreement, buying and selling or renting a home, or a contract for work. The ruling is that they must be clearly defined, and if they are valid—legally permissible—then the conditions must be fulfilled by those who are honorable. I will not belabor the point of the contract, as you can include whatever the two of you agree upon; however, please be sure your rights are protected. Make sure you do your homework on contracts in your state because the person you marry may not be the person that you have to divorce.

Case Study No. 5. "I was really in shock. This was the person that sought me out and pursued me relentlessly, said he would never be married again [I was wife no. 4], and he swore to me and anyone in earshot that this was forever and got down on one knee and proposed to me. Four years later, this was the same person that when I filed for divorce on the grounds of abandonment and desertion, the courts had to compel him to stop the attempted sale of a home we owned mutually, compel him to respond to discovery questions to my attorney, compel him to submit his bank and financial statements, compel him to pay spousal support. I had no idea who this person was. I advise women to have a marriage contract along with your state marriage license. The court process worked in my favor, but having the contract would have made it easier to protect my rights."

> O you who believe! Fulfill [your] obligations. (Al-Maidah 5:1, Al-Sharh al-Mumti', 5/241)

These are not all the red flags, but if you notice these behaviors in your courtship, it is important to discuss them with a trusted person in your life outside of his realm of manipulation. The red flags can be gray areas, but if any of these red flags show up, at the very least, set limits to protect yourself while you continue to investigate. If you find multiple red flags that cannot be cleared up, the best choice would be to just end the courtship. Remember, the narcissist has done this before. The only thing new about this is you! That is why it is easy for him to go undetected and why sometimes even the smartest, most observant sisters cannot see behind his mask. He is highly skilled at hiding in plain sight, and it is easy to fall into these gray areas when you are looking through a "love-bombed" lens. Make sure you stay in constant consultation with the trusted people in your circle.

> Prophet Muhammad (PBUH) said, "Indeed the halal [permissible] is clear and the haram [impermissible] is clear and between these two are doubtful matters that most people have no knowledge of. Whoever avoids the doubtful matters safeguards his integrity and his religion. But he who falls into doubtful matters, will eventually fall into what is haram, like a shepherd who herds his sheep too close to the sanctuary, eventually will graze therein..." (Sahih Al Bukhari and Muslim)

CHAPTER 7

Are You Trauma-Bonded?

Nevertheless, I will bring health and healing to it; I will heal my people and will let them enjoy abundant peace and security. (Bible, Jeremiah 33:6)

Mankind there has come to you a guidance from your Lord and a healing for (the diseases) in your hearts, and for those who believe, a guidance and a mercy. (Quran 10:57)

I was not sure if I should talk about the trauma bond or the steps to recovery first. However, the steps may seem overwhelming if you are trauma-bonded, so I decided to hopefully give you some insight on trauma bonding so you can look at the steps to recovery with awareness and insight.

If you missed the red flags and became a victim of manipulation, narcissistic abuse, and/or abandonment, the steps to recovery are easier said than done. However, the steps will be extremely hard steps to take if you have become trauma-bonded. Unfortunately, you do not have time to work through this process in a vacuum because you must hit the ground running to stop the damage. You must conduct triage to stop the bleeding from the knife in your back. You have to be able to simultaneously recover and fight with one arm tied behind your back. If not, by the time you recover from the emotional blow, it will be too late because the narcissist is always working deception and will not let up until you are down and unable to fight.

Trauma bonding may make you afraid, unwilling, or unable to let go of the relationship, to see him for who he truly is, or to take your life back. There are many forms of trauma bonding, but the most well-known form is Stockholm syndrome, which is also a form of PTSD. This sometimes occurs if a person was kidnapped or taken hostage and develops a sympathetic or protective relationship with their captor. This can even occur while the person is experiencing extreme physical and/or emotional abuse because trauma bonding is a coping mechanism to survive abuse.

Adults and children in emotionally and/or physically abusive relationships can experience trauma bonding. PTSD can be the result of experiencing and/or seeing a traumatic event. Abandonment is indeed a psychologically traumatic event that can result in PTSD and trauma bonding. The Mayo Clinic advises that the signs of PTSD are flashbacks, nightmares, and severe anxiety, as well as uncontrollable and persistent thoughts about the event. If you go through a traumatic event you may have temporary difficulty adjusting and coping, but with time and self-care, you will usually get better. If the symptoms last for months or years or interfere with your daily living activities, then you may have PTSD.[23]

You may continue to make excuses for and seek affection, protection, and emotional reinforcement from your abuser. You may

---

[23] Mayo Clinic, "Post-Traumatic Stress Disorder [PTSD]—Symptoms and Causes" (2022).

even become confrontational with someone who tries to assist you by pointing out the abuse or trying to remove you from the abusive situation.

"Trauma bonding is a psychological response to abuse. It occurs when the abused person forms an unhealthy bond with the person who abuses them."[24] Cycling between stage 1 (love-bombing) and stage 2 (demeaning and spirit-breaking) reinforces trauma bonding. Because you are in a perpetual cycle of receiving affection and overwhelming acts of love and kindness, then setting up and/or blaming you for some infraction, followed by silent treatment or other punishment/abuse, then back to normal behavior with love-bombing, you are kept in the "rinse and repeat" cycle. You are in an emotional tornado or washing machine, and up may look like down and left may look like right. This cycle is one of the many ways the narcissist will inflict punishment, and this also reinforces trauma bonding.

When your spouse—who may also be your main source of emotional, physical, and/or financial support—is manipulative, exploitative, or abusive, you can form unhealthy attachments as a means of survival. You may even begin to focus on the good times and ignore the manipulation and cruelty to excuse his behavior. You may hold on to thoughts of repairing the marriage that he may have already abandoned because you want to honor your commitments, but that takes two. Your trauma-bonded state can persist if you are isolated from family or friends and/or feel that you will not have support to free yourself from the relationship.

Some additional signs that you may be trauma-bonded include, but may not be limited to, ideas such as agreeing with his reasons for mistreating you, trying to cover up his mistreatment when confronted by family or friends, or not wanting to leave the manipulative and/or abusive situation. You may try to convince yourself that if you just agree with him all the time or be more appealing to him or be more available to him, then it would fix the marriage. You may rationalize that he is under a lot of pressure and will make up for his mistreatment later. You may believe that if you could just pay atten-

---

[24] Lois Zoppi, "What Is Trauma Bonding?" Medical News Today (2020).

tion to what he wanted, he wouldn't have to treat you this way or he wouldn't have abandoned the family. You may think that if you could just remember to compliment his work or appearance or thank him profusely for anything he does for you and always show gratitude for him choosing you to be his wife...the list goes on and on. Really, if you could just give more love, attention, accolades, affection, sex, adoration...then he will be happy. But remember, the "addict" can never get enough of whatever he is addicted to, and you cannot fill a bottomless pit.

These are all ideas that can indicate that you may be trauma-bonded. It is true that some of these issues and ideas are a normal part of any marriage. However, under normal circumstances, there would be a conversation and mutually agreed-upon actions to alleviate any issues. It would not be your burden to bear alone, and it would not be accompanied by the red flags and narcissistic behaviors that we discussed. Remember, Satan is an avowed enemy. You cannot bargain with him. He will never stop whispering in your ear about perceived shortcomings, and the narcissist will capitalize on any insecurities you may have developed because of his debilitating handiwork. Even if you could possibly bend your mind and body into a pretzel to provide the unconditional capitulation, adoration, physical demands, and/or constant praise that the narcissist requires, it will not result in anything better than what you have already received. In fact, he will continue to run you through the drills of "love-bombing, demeaning, and/or temporary abandonment" cycle to return and rinse and repeat the process.

The fantasy that he wants to present of the counterfeit persona and well-adjusted family will end once he knows that you actually see him for who he is. Even if you never see behind the mask, he will still leave you emotionally and/or physically while in the marriage with his right foot in and left foot outside of the marriage, living another life. That is because he is always going to seek out another supply to boost his ego. It is not only the supply but also the *new* supply that he seeks. Much like a drug addict, he will forever chase the experience of the first high that he finds in stage 1 (love-bombing). Even while he is getting the drug, literally and figuratively speaking, because the drug may even be you at the time, he will continuously seek and dream of a better drug. You cannot break this cycle, because for the untreated narcissist, this is a way of life.

Ending the trauma bond may not be as simple as just leaving the situation. Prevailing thoughts of inadequacy can continue. One of the most important things you can do to break the trauma bond is focusing on the present. Often, you may continue to reminisce about those times that were good, but now you know that these were just a means to an end. It may be tempting to wish things could have stayed that way if only…(insert any excuse). However, you must stick to reality, not the manufactured life that was presented to you, not the stage play that you were living. You must accept that you only met the authentic person during stage 3 (abandonment/discard). You must accept that the person that you thought that you were bonding with was the "publicity agent" presented to you in stage 1 (love-bombing). The charming, attentive man seeking family life that you met in stage 1 (love-bombing) does not really exist; he is a character on a stage.

You probably found many holes and/or red flags in his accounts of his childhood, his life as an adult, as a husband, and as a father. There were likely gaps and things that just did not add up in every aspect of his life. Ask yourself a question, Would you really want to live a life like the one you had indefinitely? Not the love-bombed life but the life that you were living on eggshells, waiting for another unexplained mood swing, another unexplained absence, another outburst, another deception, another act of sabotage, another lie or manipulated and orchestrated argument. This is not the life that Allah intended for you. Think about that manipulated life, and you will be in the reality of what your life would have been in year 10, 20, and even in year 30 of this marriage. You must accept that this relationship, for him, was never meant to be long-term. If you check his track record, you will likely be able to confirm this.

Case Study No. 1. "After he ghosted me, I discovered that he had done the same thing to several other women. I spoke to women whose friends had sat with my former intended. It was revealed that he would ask the women to marry him, tell them to start looking for apartments for them to move into, then abruptly stopped communicating with them and ignored them if he saw them in public."

Case Study No. 5. "After the abandonment, I shockingly discovered that he pretty much did the same thing to a previous spouse. He abruptly left the marriage, and my engagement ring was in their house. I had no idea."

Take note: did you see him working toward any of those mutual goals that he shared with you during the love-bombing stage? Look with clear eyes now that the love-bombing cycle cannot be reinjected to distract you from the truth. Did he leave behind any evidence of this work that the two of you discussed during love-bombing? Has this relationship left you in a deficit mentally, physically, spiritually, and/or financially? If the two of you did have any financial or material success, did he take it or attempt to take it with him as he scurried off to where he came from or to his newly reinvented life?

To break the trauma bond, you must focus on the facts of what happened. Abandonment is not an answer to ending a marriage. Do not delude yourself and spend time reminiscing. Do not be hard on yourself because this will keep you trauma-bonded. Be kind to yourself. You are healing, and you deserve to be happy. And you *will* be happy once again.

Case Study No. 1. "I was very emotionally off-balanced for months. I am currently in ongoing therapy. I was questioning my self-worth to the point of thinking, *Why wasn't I good enough to be selected? Why wasn't I a choice? Was I not pretty enough?* I couldn't find joy in my regular activities, such as my job of teaching. I withdrew from the active life I maintained. No matter where I was, I was thinking about the abandonment, what he did to me, how unworthy I felt, that I was not going to have a good life. There are no good men in the world. There is nobody that can be good to me."

Case Study No. 2. "To this day after three years, I still have trauma and anxiety when I think about all that I went through and the deception and manipulation I was subjected to… I continue to experience recurring dreams now and then. I feel like I was in a war. It has been three years, and his name or seeing certain things still evokes trauma. His friends, family, and colleagues have no idea of what he was capable of."

Case Study No. 3. "During the marriage, he left for weeks, and I began to panic. I did not know what was wrong. Of course, I went and tried to figure it all out. He would make up excuses, saying he was going through some things. That was the first sign of the drop from the high to the extreme low. It caused me a lot of anxiety and confusion. And then he brought it right back around to love-bombing maybe about a week later. That was just the first time."

Case Study No. 4. "My self-worth diminished to next to nothing. I was very anxious and afraid that he would come back and physically hurt me. I was prescribed antidepressants to help me get through the divorce proceedings and the first months away from him."

Case Study No. 5. "My anxiety level was extremely high because I had entrusted my son to the person that took both of us on a vacation and abandoned us there. We had even left the country with this person. I could not eat or sleep for months because I was plagued with thoughts and nightmares of my son's traumatic reaction to the abandonment. His reaction was constantly replaying in my head day and night. I thought I must be a bad mother to expose my son to this trauma. I was overwhelmed with feelings of being unsafe. I could not dismiss the thought that if I was unable to see that this person was unsafe, then what other dangers am I missing in my life every day?"

To regain your confidence and security, use positive reinforcement and self-care. Increase your attention on your healing and development and not on the abuse or the abuser. Another way to break this trauma bond is to learn about narcissistic abuse and abandonment, trauma bonding, and toxic relationships. No one wants to be in a toxic relationship. You were most likely manipulated with acts of kindness and false promises to lure you into the relationship.

Once you learn how to recognize this behavior, you will empower yourself and be able to protect yourself in the future. You have learned a great deal during your trauma. You have learned several red-flag behaviors; you have learned that the narcissist lacks empathy and impulse control and therefore cannot be trusted with your well-being or that of your children. You have learned that you were living in a house of cards and a relationship that lacked true honesty, empathy, or intent for longevity. You have also learned that since he is always seeking the "next high," you were never on an even playing field. But your true worth and your true strength are not tied to him. Use this knowledge, wisdom, and understanding to your advantage, and share what you have learned to spare others this sort of abuse.

Let's put and keep things in perspective. Stay in the present and reality of what he has done. The premeditated abandonment and/or abuse made it impossible to protect yourself and/or your children from the sudden trauma of an unplanned separation or divorce. All those affected can be traumatized and/or trauma-bonded. It may even cause you to become doubtful of current relationships that may have been years in the making. Anxiety, distrust, and anger may negatively affect these previously stable relationships if you remain in the trauma-bonded state.

If left untreated, trauma bonding can result in short- or long-term abandonment issues. This is a type of distress and anxiety with creating new relationships after experiencing trauma. "While abandonment trauma seems to be more common in the developing years of childhood and early adulthood, the experiences that cause abandonment trauma can happen at any stage in life. Adults may be traumatized by abandonment as a consequence of an unplanned divorce or the loss of a spouse or partner. The termination of these most essential connections can make a person feel unsafe, unloved, and unprepared to have meaningful future relationships."[25]

Being denied the right to your emotions and expressing your feelings, especially when dealing with narcissistic manipulation, can place an excessive amount of stress on you to be perfect under manipulation. Ask yourself, Was I avoiding outbursts by constantly "putting on a good face," ignoring my own emotional and physical needs? This type of suppression can have damaging consequences for current and new relationships. "Fear of being unable to protect yourself as an adult because you weren't protected as a child can make

---

[25] The Balance 2022, https://balanceluxuryrehab.com/.

you distrust others. Fear of guilt from past mistakes cause you to choose people who don't meet your basic standards. Fear causes you to disregard the feedback of friends and family. Fear keeps you in a relationship you don't want to be in…"[26]

Seeking spiritual and professional counseling is paramount to recovery. Don't go at it alone! If you had a traumatic car accident that left you with a broken leg, wouldn't you seek medical help or would you let time heal your wounds and possibly have a permanent limp or ongoing pain? This injury is no different. Your spirit and your psyche have both experienced a traumatic injury that needs urgent professional attention. It's a scientific fact that emotional trauma—like physical trauma—changes you! Your thought patterns, sense of safety, reactions to your environment and the people around you are hypersensitive. Get professional help so you can have a full recovery—mental, physical, spiritual, emotional, and financial.

At this point, you may be asking yourself, How can I avoid attracting another person like him in the future? The narcissists are attracted to people who have qualities or possessions that he can drain. The person that is able to replenish themselves after spirit-breaking cycles is also a good pick because it will take a while to drain the supply. He will also be attracted to problem-solvers who are full of empathy and sympathy for others. This is because he is a master at alternating between playing the hero or the victim, which ever benefits him at the time. Remember, he told you, "My ex-wife, mother, siblings, children, supervisor, coworkers don't understand/respect/love me as I should be…" Blah blah blah. He will drain you mentally, physically, spiritually, and/or financially, and then he will flip the script and play the victim of you. He will go to these same people that he complained about to you, but in the new version, you are the one who is not giving him the due respect, adoration, or attention that he demands.

He will also be attracted to people who are successful and have a well-rounded life with family and friends and community members. This will aid him in developing a persona of being a family- or

---

[26] Clay and Clay, *Selection Perfection*.

community-oriented person, and this helps him learn how to imitate empathy. This also creates a cover for him to hide his true intentions and likely a secret life. He will also be attracted to people who are successful in business/careers, with family or in the religious or secular community. This is because he covets this reputation or wants to expand his reputation by using you as proof that he is worthy of this adoration. "Sweetheart, we will be a power couple" or "Let me invest in your business, education, or dreams of [insert whatever your dream is]."

The best way to stop attracting the narcissist is to put up clear boundaries. Now that you know the red flags, listen to your intuition when the red flags are waving at you or when something just doesn't feel right or feels too good to be true. Refuse to move too fast; do not let him sweep you away in the current, head over heels into oblivion. Don't let anyone whisk you down the aisle to marriage.

Iyanla Vanzant said that while there are many times when things will just fall into place, you cannot depend on free-falling your way through life. This is the go-to of the manipulator: to present a good option so you can effortlessly free-fall your way into a blissful marriage without the hard work of preparation. Do your *homework*! You owe it to yourself. But if you set boundaries and are unavailable for a whirlwind courtship and marriage, if he is a manipulator or out for instant gratification, he will find another victim, because instant and quick gratification is his goal. Please learn to love yourself, which can be hard for the natural caregiver. In this process, you must put your need for clarity above all else before making any decisions. Take the time to gift yourself clarity. If not, he will use your distractions to run circles around you, plotting your demise. You will be ripe for sabotage.

Break the habits of being attracted to these types of people. On the surface and in the beginning, they are very charismatic, outgoing, confident, and caring. It will be hard to resist this type of personality with these admirable traits; however, you must analyze and factor in the red flags that point to manipulation and abandonment. Once you determine that these flags are present, you must overlook those supposed good traits, at least temporarily, while you investigate the red flags. Peek under the mask, because with this personality type, these good characteristics are all a means to an end, which, for the narcissist, is always to drain you while causing you potentially lifelong injury with deception, infidelity, emotional and/or physical abuse, and/or abandonment.

In their book *Selection Perfection*, Hasan and Naa'ila Clay talk about the issue of being attracted to the type of person that is extremely committed to their personal dreams and passions. You admire the way the person loves and is dedicated to their career or community service; however, this passion never seems to translate to their love for you. The person is committed to their dreams but nothing else.[27] The white-knight narcissist is the personality type that will seem dedicated to very noble causes in the community and have a profession that involves helping people on the surface. He may always seem to be a selfless giver, but make no mistake, he is always making sure that his acts are witnessed by the right people to build his counterfeit persona.

Be aware of any old wounds you have from childhood and adulthood. Work on overcoming and healing them so you can protect yourself from future abuse. If the plane is going down, all experts agree to put the oxygen mask on yourself before helping others. The narcissist will use their mask and rip your mask from your hands all while playing the victim. Please memorize the flags, and do not turn away for fear of disappointment about what you may find. When you watch a scary movie or thriller and the lady goes to open the door or she peeps under the bed or checks what is rumbling in the shed out back, you scream, "Stop! Don't go in there!" Well, doing your homework on him may feel just as scary. It may feel like you are going to ruin this great future that he has described, but you *must* open that door, pull back the curtain, and look under the mask. If it exposes the great future that Allah has planned for you, you will breathe a sigh of relief, and you will say, "All praise to God [Alhamdulillah]." However, if it exposes an evil plot, a den of

---

[27] Clay and Clay, *Selection Perfection*.

deception, then you will still breathe a sigh of relief, and you will still say, "All praise to God [Alhamdulillah]!"

The flags provided in this book speak mostly to the initial courtship, but there are many other flags that can appear after the marriage or in other relationships and friendships. You may now recognize some of these unwanted behaviors in family members, friends, and colleagues, as well as members of your religious community. You don't need to walk around paranoid with a black light, but do please remove your good-natured blinders! Narcissists do not seek out people who are skilled at standing their ground and protecting their own interests no matter what. They also have no defenses against people whose intuition is high, who are clairvoyant, because these people are emotionally gifted and can spot the narcissist a mile away. The narcissist has no use for nor has any strength against this type of person. You can acquire this skill. I am not saying that you don't have your own best interests at heart, but if you are a constant caregiver, you have no problem putting yourself last. Again, do not change your kind and good-hearted, selfless ways. Keep your loving, caring heart. These qualities are a gift. You have offered the right thing but just to the wrong person. Become like the daylily. These beautiful flowers are hard as nails. As delicate as they are, they can withstand freezing temperatures and other harsh weather conditions, but they come back to bloom year after year.

The survival of the fittest is not only referring to the physically fit but also to the intellectually and emotionally fit, so let's get fit! Even this trauma is an exercise to strengthen you for the next test because there is always a next test. You will keep getting the same test until you pass, and then there will be the next test. You can't have a testimony without a test! You must seek this knowledge to survive the many ways Satan will use those around you to sabotage family life.

If you feel you must have sympathy for their disorder, please do it from far away. But in all honesty, you really should save your sympathy for someone that will care because the narcissist will not care about your sympathy and will not care about changing or making amends. He will only care about finding the next supply. You must disengage and end the trauma bond!

You will be amazed at your strength after you have emerged from the tunnel that, at one point, was so dark. You will look back and no longer be able to see beyond that point where there was no light. That is because you will have finally emerged, and you will be standing in the light! Look back at what you have accomplished! Look at how the test of adversity has strengthened you! Be proud of yourself! It is okay to be happy; it is okay to be proud of your accomplishments.

CHAPTER 8

Reclaim Your Life!

> But if they intend to deceive you-then sufficient for you is Allah. It is He who supported you with His help and with the believers. (Quran 8:62)

The previous chapters covered a great deal about the narcissist and his effect on the family and the community and how to spot the red flags and protect yourself. Unfortunately, even the best-laid plans can still fall short and land you in a love-bomb/demean/abandon/ trauma-bonded cycle.

So you missed the flags or saw them and thought you could help him or change him during the marriage, and now you find yourself deep in the muck of things! You may wonder at this point why a believer would use these tactics. Remember, this is at its core a mental health issue that presents as manipulation for personal gain. He was at times two steps ahead because he came with an agenda that you might not have seen until months or years later. Using the desire to get married to further your *deen* or to meet religious obligations, to start a family, or to grow as a couple made you vulnerable and was a good cover for him.

If you are a victim of this abuse, as with any other abuse, you should seek support in your family and religious community. However, if you encounter obstacles there, reach out beyond your circle. Remember, abandonment is *not* your fault. In this and other cases of abuse, women are prone to blaming themselves and wondering, *What did I do wrong? What could I have done better? Why didn't I see the signs?*

> Prophet Muhammad (PBUH) said, "Being so kind, polite and cheerful toward the women of the world holds no value when we cannot be such to our own wives, sisters, and mothers." (Mufti Ismail Menk)

> Now if you show kindness and faithfulness to my master, tell me; and if not, tell me so I may know which way to turn. (The Holy Bible, Genesis 24:49)

Seek justice! Allah/God has forbidden all forms of injustice. There are three levels of injustice:

1. *Al-shirk*, the highest level of injustice is associating partners with Allah, such as idol worship.
2. Committing sins, which is being unjust toward yourself.
3. *Dhulm* or being unjust toward others, whether human beings or other creatures. Think about that! Even Allah's creatures are assured justice, so how can you be exempt from this privilege?

When you start to seek justice, he will become enraged. To paraphrase Marcus Garvey, when you stand up and become upright, the people riding your back will scream the loudest as they are falling from their position of comfort! This person is manipulating, mistreating, and abusing you. When you fight back, he will say that you are being ungrateful for all that he has given you, well, what he took and allowed you to have of your dignity. He will say that you are sabotaging his manufactured reputation and, thus, you are the aggressor. He will play the victim because you have failed to meet the expectations of providing ongoing accolades or of being the rug placed beneath him on which he can walk and wipe his feet!

He will lie to everyone around him, including himself, to make himself the victim. How dare you fight back? Who are you to defy him? Why does he think this way? He thinks this way because he feels entitled to everything: your love, your admiration, your respect, and your dignity. Entitled people believe that they are also allowed to mistreat you and be the victim when you have the audacity to protest. This is because he is void of true empathy and compassion that is for anything beyond his own wants and needs. And what does he want and need more than anything? The illusion of a stellar reputation, superficial success, attention, accolades, and a sense of power.

If you are a victim of abandonment, which is surely an injustice, it is very important to seek justice for yourself and regain control of your life. Your life has been turned upside down, shaking out and revealing an engagement or marriage of opportunity. You must work fast and meticulously to set things back on the right path for your mental, spiritual, and financial well-being.

This will be a traumatic time for you. You will have a huge desire to lay down or to check out from all communications. It's understandable because your spirit has been attacked by a parasitic infection, and you must remedy this with prayer and action! Prayer without action will not work for any situation and definitely not for this fight to reclaim your life. Of all of Allah's creatures, we are the only creatures with intellect, so use it now to rid yourself of the parasite!

Don't lay down...*work*! Unfortunately, if you check out at this point, it may cause a downward spiral from which it may be difficult to recover. Let's face it. Something of this magnitude can change the course of your life, but it does not have to change it for the worse! Just buckle up, *sistahs*! It's going to be a bumpy ride, *but* you *will* be able to restore your life and come out on the other side stronger and smarter than ever. But first, you must take these *immediate actions*, which includes, but are not limited to, the following and not necessarily in this order:

1. *Assess Your Spiritual Foundation*

> Anas ibn Maalik said: "Whenever something distressed him, the Prophet Muhammad used to say: 'Oh Ever-Living, Oh Self-Sustaining, by Your mercy I seek Your help." (Reported by al-Tirmidhi, no. 3446)

> Have I not commanded you? Be strong and of good courage; do not be afraid, nor be dismayed, for the Lord your God is with you wherever you go. (The Bible, Joshua 1:9, NKJV)

Lean on your faith, your family, and your religious community. This will be your strength. Do not fall into the trap of asking, "Why did Allah do this to me?"

Be determined to grow and expand your faith during this time. Being sad, frustrated, angry, and afraid and having some really hard days do not mean that you lack faith or that you are slipping into disbelief. It only means that you are human. Give yourself a break! Give yourself many breaks. Make sure you do not fall into despair where you begin to doubt that Allah is in control of all things. Even in the darkest of times, still believe that Allah is in full control, because those who turn to Allah in times of distress receive greater rewards.

Do not turn to other means of relief from your distress because that will be counterproductive to your spiritual, emotional, physical, and/or financial growth. Without a doubt, as sure as you are walking and breathing, while you are in distress, many of these counterproductive options will be presented to you openly or covertly as Satan is always whispering in your ear. It may come in the form of a person from your past who will pop up out of the woodworks or whispers from Satan to just indulge in frivolous things as a distraction to relieve your distress, such as hanging out, overeating, shopping or other time-wasting activities. Stay the course and patiently persevere, because indulging in these distractions will take you further away from your healing. These distractions will likely leave you with yet another injury from which you will need to recover, but worse, because this time, it will be self-inflicted! Do not overestimate your spiritual strength and strike out alone. If you can help it, do not miss congregational services, reading or praying, or even social activities with your family and religious community. Hold *tight* to the rope of Allah and your religion and religious community! Do not leave the religion! Remember, when Prophet Musa/Moses went to confront the Egyptian king, he asked Allah to allow his brother Harun/Aaron to accompany him to help him and to strengthen him. Ask your Creator to provide help to you from among family, friends, and community members.

> And serve your Lord until death overtakes
> you. (Hijr 99)

This is the time to reevaluate your spiritual foundation. Were there any cracks in your practice of the religion that allowed him to take advantage of your trust? Were you isolated in some way from the religious community or family? Did you ignore or miss signs that he was not sincere in his practice of the religion? Did you miss or ignore acts of hypocrisy? And if so, evaluate the reasons you would have missed and/or ignored these flags. This is not shifting the blame to you. At this point, you must assess the weaknesses in your fortitude that allowed him to manipulate you instead of strengthening you in the religion as a husband should. Accessing these weaknesses will allow you to create a solid corrective action plan when moving forward.

There are times in everyone's life where you may be distracted and not guarding your faith. The most vulnerable times are in times of loneliness, a change in your life, such as work, moving to a new city, or an illness. In addition, the death of a loved one, stress, and fatigue (mental, physical, and spiritual), and of course, love-bombing can all cause you to lose sight of guarding your faith/belief. Take stock in your faith and God-consciousness, and your daily practice to see what needs to be shored up, because another test is coming when extracting the narcissist from your life.

If you do not guard your thoughts, you will begin to judge yourself for not seeing the danger. "Fear leads you to doubt your intuition. What if you're wrong about the suggestions your gut is giving you to walk away? The unwarranted misgivings you implant mentally speak to you in the form of judgement."[28] You need to move from this spot where you may find yourself frozen mentally and physically from the inhumane, blindsided blow to the back of your head. Sisters, you are tired and emotionally battered and bruised at this point, but do not distress for too long because there is work to do, so let's get to it!

> I seek refuge in Allah/God and in His Power from the evil of what I find and of what I guard against. (The Holy Quran 243)

> Be strong and courageous. Do not be afraid or terrified because of them, for the LORD your God goes with you; he will never leave you nor forsake you. (The Holy Bible, Deuteronomy 31:6)

2. *Inform Your Family and Religious Community Leadership*

> He who believes in Allah and the Last Day, let him maintain good relations with kins. (Al Bukhari and Muslim)

> But if anyone does not provide for his relatives, and especially for members of his house-

---

[28] Clay and Clay, *Selection Perfection*.

hold, he has denied the faith and is worse than
an unbeliever. (The Holy Bible, 1 Timothy 5:8)

Knowledge is *power*! Some victims of abuse are abused for quite
a while before anyone knows about it, and unfortunately, in the case
of psychological abuse, you, the abused, are sometimes unaware in
the beginning. You may be unaware because you are being cycled
between fogs of love-bombing, demeaning, and gaslighting. You
may not see the abuse except in hindsight after the abandonment
when the process is broken. That is because there will be no cycle of
love-bombing to manipulate you back into denial.

Do not hide what he has done because this is just what he is
hoping you will do so he can keep up his persona. Hiding the situation will lead to even more stress, if imaginable. Remember, he
likely ran a smear campaign behind your back in stage 2 (demean-
ing/spirit-breaking). You may not be able to reach out to some of
your mutual friends or his family because the manipulation ran deep.
For weeks or months, he has been spinning untruths about you, so
they will not come to your aid. Do not let this deter you. You will
find that those whom you thought would step forward will be afraid.
Some people are not built for battle, but they are still good people
and want to support you. Make no mistake about it. It is a battle
when going up against someone as unscrupulous as an abandoning
narcissist. He will be a master manipulator and expert liar and will
have no boundaries. And no low will be too low! If you do not fight
for your rights, then who will? Furthermore, if you do not stand up,
you cannot heal.

You will also be surprised by some people that you had not
imagined would come to your aid. They will march onto the bat-
tlefield in front of you, beside you, and pushing you from behind.
Allah knows best! You are loved by many people. These bonds of
family, community, and friends were established long before you met
him. *This is your base!* They will support you spiritually, mentally,
physically, and financially if you need it, because you have never cut
family and community ties. Allah will bless you for that. Allow them

to assist you with your children as well. The children will need a support system that goes beyond just you.

3.   Seek Family Counseling

Tragically, your children have also been traumatized. Seek a specialist for them, whether they were his biological children or not. You will all need to talk a whole lot about your fears, devastation, and anger. Yes! You will and can be angry. It is a natural response. However, do not let the anger go unchecked. It was reported that Prophet Muhammad (PBUH) was angered by seeing injustice and oppression, but you must try to breathe so you can think and work to recover.

> Aslam reported that 'Umar Ibin al Khattab said, "Do not let your love become dependency, nor allow your anger to become destructive." (Hadith 1329, narrated by 'Ad al Razzaq)

You may have developed some, if not all, of the symptoms of PTSD. PTSD does not just affect those who suffered physical abuse or some sort of wartime trauma. It is also found in victims of emotional and psychological abuse. Prayer and talking to family and friends will help. However, a licensed and experienced therapist can facilitate your journey through PTSD, if applicable, and the stages of grief. This therapy will be a huge part of your recovery.

According to Dr. Jean Collins in her clinical experience, there are some hard-to-treat cases of PTSD because of five extenuating circumstances:

- Multiple traumatic incidents without time or opportunity to process or recover between them *(The phycological abuse and then the abandonment are multiple injuries.)*
- Moral injury—when something contradicts our moral code *(Abandonment is definitely a moral injury.)*

- Disbelief—trauma followed by disbelief or lack of support from others *(The narcissist's counterfeit persona and smear campaign can prevent others from believing the abuse.)*
- Trauma that involves the senses—sight, hearing, smell, such as the smell of burned bodies
- Functional PTSD—when it becomes a coping mechanism and a normal state of being or functioning *(This can look like trauma bonding and/or developing abandonment issues.)*

Some narcissists will attempt to return to inflict more pain and keep you in a perpetual trauma-bonded cycle. If you were able to see behind his mask and spot the lies and hypocrisy, he is not likely to return. However, if he abandoned while you were still in a period of adoration, he might come back to toy with your emotional state for his own deviant satisfaction. If you are lucky, he will leave once and for all, and you can begin the healing process uninterrupted.

Forgive yourself for not seeing the signs and for unknowingly allowing this type of abuse. Keep walking away with your head up! Literally. Studies show that moving your body in a forward motion is instrumental in healing emotionally. Taking a walk daily will reduce stress and allow you to clear your mind. It sounds so simple that you will be tempted to skip this step. But the simplicity and ease of it is the blessing from your Creator! He has given you this simple method to rejuvenate your mind and your body!

4. *Seek Legal Advice*

For Muslims, the Quran is the principal source of Islamic law, likewise for Christians, the Bible, and for Jews, the Torah. You are allowed and should seek legal assistance if what we are seeking is not in conflict with the religion. Hopefully, you were able to secure a marriage contract or prenuptial agreement that met the requirements of the religion and of your state. Remember, it must meet both to fully protect your rights, and hopefully, you have obtained a state marriage license. These combined can provide ultimate protection from him as it is clear by the act of abandonment that he will not honor his religious obligations. You can find a sample of both in the appendices. If you opted out of the marriage contract in stage 1 (love-bombing), you still need to get legal advice ASAP! Do not try to be your own attorney even if you *are* an attorney because your emotional state will be a barrier!

Many women who are victims of abandonment are at risk of losing their homes, transportation, even their jobs after overwhelming financial and emotional distress. If you cannot afford an attorney, check with legal aid and/or family members for assistance. Also check with your masjid, church, or abandonment/divorce support groups that can make referrals. Abandonment and desertion are legally different. Abandonment is leaving without warning, and desertion is removing financial support in the process. Check the definitions in your state and create a plan with your attorney.

The narcissist is very cunning. He will absolutely use the legal system to shirk his duties of maintenance and support of the family. He will now lean on the separation of "church and state." You can overcome this hurdle. For example, if your attorney is not a Muslim, you must quickly educate him/her about your rights as a Muslim woman. They may first just focus on your rights as a citizen of the state, but if you are a member and citizen of the Muslim community and hopefully have an enforceable Islamic marriage contract, then that also needs to be enforced. Some states have precedents set on Islamic spousal support. Muslim women, by way of the Quran and Sunnah, are entitled to twelve months of maintenance/spousal support upon separation or divorce. Unfortunately, there are blogs that tell men how to go about avoiding spousal support by advising them to avoid the state license and marriage contracts. But let's face the facts. At this point, he is no longer operating from the foundation of a believer. Nevertheless, you want to introduce this information into the court even if just for documentation. The more we do this, the closer we will be to Muslim women having their rights enforced. You can get approval for the Imam that married you to testify in court about your rights as a Muslim woman, but if your Imam is too afraid to step up, you can get any Imam. He will still be seen as an expert witness.

Think about this. How can you have the freedom to practice your religion in this country and make life-changing decisions based on your religion, but your religion is locked out of the courtroom when it's time to litigate those decisions? Make sure your attorney and/or investigator (yes, investigator) determine the new residence and subpoenas his bank statements, employment records, and any other information that will prove that this was a premeditated act. They can also determine if he is hiding finances or diverted finances away from the home/marriage while building his secret life. The diversion of finances, joint or separate, is also an actionable offense. You must also be meticulous in your own documentation. Criminals always make mistakes, because if they were smart, they would not be criminals. All these things can help in obtaining maintenance/support even if you outearn him. They will try to use this, but don't back off. The law is not that cut and dry.

If you share children, it is important to negotiate support and visitation. Do not prevent visitation unless there are legal grounds that require this step. If you must exchange the children for visitation, use a third party so you can stay out of his reach. Do not give him access to you alone because this could be an opening for a love-bombing or manipulation tactic to keep you from asking for and obtaining your full rights or just another opportunity to demean you. If you must communicate, do so in writing, using email to document all communications. Remember, if it is not in writing, it did not happen! Do not be tempted to communicate via telephone or in person with him, because just like the liar and manipulator that he is, he will use this as an opportunity to create further chaos and/or further abuse you! Work through the attorney and counselors to devise a plan that works for you and your children.

5. *Touch Base with Your Medical Doctor*

Emotional and psychological distress can easily lead to physical illness. Get in touch with your medical doctor or urgent care clinic if you are experiencing any of the following: nausea when eating, inability to eat, overeating, weight loss or weight gain, headaches,

heart palpitations from anxiety, raised blood pressure, excessive tired-
ness, muscle aches and pains, or poor quality of sleep. These are just
some of the symptoms that could indicate depression and/or PTSD.
Your doctor can determine your emotional and physical state and/
or refer you to a specialist for counseling and treatment. Be sure
to document this information for court. Also, talk to your medical
practitioner about testing to be safe, because his alternate or hidden
life could have included women, drugs, or even homosexuality as
narcissists are prone to substance abuse and sex addictions.

6. *Expose the Abuse*

Speak truth to power! Speaking out against injustice is not only
your right but your responsibility!

If you don't speak out, others in your community may suffer the
same fate. Do not let others suffer while you are silent, especially if
you have the means to speak up. There are, of course, some abusive
situations that leave women unable to speak out for fear of their
safety, and it would be ill-advised to put yourself or your children in
danger.

You have given up enough power, so be careful about who and
what you give power to outside of your Creator. Take your power
back by exposing the truth because his goal is to throw the rock and
hide his hand. Therefore, you must speak the truth to free yourself
of this trauma bond. Some will tell you to be quiet, but Allah has
already given you the right to speak out. Those who want you to be
quiet may be attempting to preserve his counterfeit persona and preserve their own reputation if they were a part of or also participated
in this type of behavior. They also may be trying to preserve the
reputation of the community or may just be unaware of your rights.
Remember, you only have the rights that you are aware of! But let's
face it. The best way to preserve the reputation of the community is
to prevent and stop injustice of any kind. There are some men who
will not have the courage to speak out against this or any injustice for
that matter. But rest assured, there are other men who will step in the

lion's den with you because they are men who hate the oppression of women!

Sisters, you are strong! Remember, there is nothing to fear in this world but Allah. If the leaders are weak in your community, find a fearless leader from another community to fight this fight with you! I am not saying that you cannot do it alone; there are many things that sisters can do alone. However, sometimes it defies common sense. You may be emotional, which is normal under these extreme circumstances, and the support person can be a cooler head until you recover from the blow you have suffered. Your support person can also be a physical presence as well because some narcissists can be violent. But if you must go at it alone, remember, Allah and His angels are always with you!

7. *Keep Your Head Up!*

You have dodged a bullet, whether early or late in the relationship. Do not entertain people who seek to place this burden on you. Do not let them force you to explain his actions of which you were not a part of nor had prior knowledge of, because these people likely lack the courage to stand up for the rights of women anyway. They will look for reasons to absolve him of this egregious action. This can sometimes unfortunately include the authorities among you in your community. You have too much work to do to entertain cowards! If they are not willing to fight for the rights of women and children, then what are they willing to fight for?

I cannot stress this enough: spend a good deal of time outside, even if it is just your front porch or backyard. Go for walks and find quiet places and beautiful scenery to take in; put these in your line of vision. The *sun has healing properties*! Do not hide out in your home. Bask in the light of the sun! Allah is going to see, hear, and respond to your call for justice.

Surely, Allah (God) is with those who are as-sabirun—the patient. (Quran 8:46)

> This is my command—be strong and cou-
> rageous! Do not be afraid or discouraged. For the
> LORD your God is with you wherever you go.
> (The Holy Bible, Joshua 1:9)

Develop a new focus in your life by taking on new hobbies, projects, an exercise regimen, and/or meaningful activities that help others. Helping those less fortunate will improve your outlook, and there is always someone less fortunate than you despite your current circumstances. These activities can also lead to increased social support. Reconnect with family and friends with whom you lost touch while the narcissist was wreaking havoc in your life. Surround yourself and your children with positive male role models. Do not make sweeping judgments about men. Real men do not participate in these activities, and they can be a support system.

No matter what the struggle, be faithful and patient. Allah has promised a reward for you in this life and the next. This stage of your recovery and restoration will not look like perfect composure. You will have good days and some very, very bad days. And even during those times, you will still maintain your faith and your God-consciousness. Do not give up on the institution of marriage. Prophet Muhammad said, "There is no institution in Islam that is more sacred than the institution of marriage."

8. *Learn How to Repel the Narcissist*

You may have been conditioned to withstand or tolerate the narcissist because you were raised with a parent or other history of dealing, unknowingly, with a narc. Believe it or not, all this chaos occurred in my life while I was caring for my terminally ill father in our home, so I was deep in the thick of things and operating in survival mode daily. Therefore, this level of stress being my father's primary caregiver clouded my vision, because when you are in a tornado, you cannot tell the ground from the sky. I was being manipulated while I was looking in the other direction. In addition, after being abandoned by my husband, my father passed away just six weeks later. I read about narcissistic manipulation and abuse and realized I was experiencing these behaviors but was completely unable to see it because of taking care of my dad, son, and husband and working full-time. Unfortunately, I didn't have a name to put to it and didn't have knowledge of the narcissistic pattern of abuse and behavior until I was educated by a fellow survivor and received professional counseling and therapy. If you have/had a parent that used manipulative behaviors, you can be predispositioned to withstand or overlook these behaviors, which plays right into the hands of the narcissist.

For example, I am basically seen as a confident person; I have a spiritual base and center; I have a good circle of family, friends, and colleagues; I am considered well educated and accomplished professionally; and I am an extrovert. I am no wallflower, and I have never needed a fainting couch. However, in retrospect, it seems that as confident as I thought I was, I was not confident enough to set and enforce reasonable boundaries, coupled with not knowing, really being ignorant of, the red flags. I cannot count how many times I ignored my "gut," which was a sign of lacking confidence to exert myself in this situation. This was a recipe for disaster that could not have had any other outcome really. This is an example of knowing the role that I played and that it is not the same as blaming myself. Of course, I did not have ill intent against myself; I just lacked the knowledge I needed to fully protect myself against the ever-cunning and always manipulative narcissist.

If you have low self-esteem and/or tend to deny your own needs to care for others, this can be a crack in your fortitude. Low self-esteem or the inability to exert and protect yourself doesn't show up the same in every person. It doesn't mean that you are not a capable person or that you do not care about yourself. Even feeling good about yourself but allowing others to take advantage of your kindness is an issue because you are trying to please others at your own expense. Of course, I am not a psychologist, just relying on some mother wit and lessons learned from my own bumps and bruises.

Remember, the narcissist is a *professional* at pumping and gassing you up to make you think they adore you in the love-bombing stage. This is to get you to let your guard down, and as sure as the "big road runs through Georgia," he will attack mentally, spiritually, and/or physically while you are basking in the light of love-bombing or caring for parents, children, or even him. You are looking into the sun and can't see your hand right in front of your own face! Eyes wide shut! So your confidence must be shored up so you can protect yourself.

So how do you repel the narcissist in the future? It would be quite nice if you could just hang a rope of garlic around your neck or set out a rat trap full of cheese, but life is not that easy! You must use your litmus test of the red flags we discussed and *set boundaries!* *Narcissists hate boundaries* because they really believe that the world and you belong to them to do with what they will. Unfortunately, you cannot successfully set and reinforce boundaries unless you shore up your confidence, which may not be as simple as you think.

Girls are typically groomed to be pleasers. Parents mean well, but look at your family structure or someone around you. The girl that is the oldest is typically raised to be a caregiver and to be a "mini me" to the mother. Even if she is second in line, the boy is not groomed to be a caregiver. She is still groomed to be a second mother even to the older brother, catering to his needs. This, by itself, is not a terrible thing in what should be the safety of the family unit. But in the wrong hands, like the narcissist, this is a setup for hardship in life, at work, and in relationships because she will default to catering to others and not herself.

Not exposing your children, especially girls, to the good things that life has to offer sets them up to have low expectations. For example, I happened to be with a group of children at an outing that was a treat but a typical family outing for most. One of the young teenage girls turned to me and said, "This is the best thing that I have ever experienced in my life!" I was almost brought to tears because it was something that many people do regularly. I thought, if some snotty-nosed boy smoking a vape with his pants hanging to his knees shows her something just a bit more than this, she could be swept up in a New York minute! May Allah protect us all. Parents, do not feed your girls to the narcissists! Shore them up with spiritual strength, confidence, and real talk! Sugarcoating and beating around the bush is dangerous! Make it plain.

Boundaries! Boundaries! Boundaries! Set and enforce reasonable boundaries. Please teach your daughters to do the same; it is never too late to start, so start *today*! This includes, but is not limited to, boundaries with your time, money, emotions, body, finances, even your sympathy. Set boundaries with giving out your sympathy because the forever-victimized narcissist will pray on your sympathy to create the "flying monkey" scenario and turn you against others to protect him all while he is abusing you. Sometimes you must have sympathy from "over yonder" across the room, but keep it moving! Setting reasonable boundaries does not mean to shift to distrust and hate all men or people in general. That is just "wayyyyy tew merch"! It means setting expectations of yourself and those around you for the treatment and care of your mental, physical, and spiritual safety and general well-being. Anyone—family, friends, and the man looking to share your life—should respect your boundaries. Now since this may be a "new you," it can take some practice on your part. Also, some of those around you will wince and feel uncomfortable and complain because you are removing them from their place of comfort, but they will get used to your boundaries, or they will go away. Either way, your problem will be solved! Voilà! These and other things should be considered when learning to repel the narcissist. But, sistah, maybe get that garlic necklace and rat trap with cheese for backup!

CHAPTER 9

Buckle Up, Sistahs! It's Going to Be a Bumpy Ride!

Talk about your experience, and you will find, as unconscionable as it is, that many others have experienced this trauma. They may have remained quiet until *you* spoke up and gave them courage. I have had women in the store, at the bank, at work—everywhere imaginable—telling me their stories, but not until I spoke up! Expose the abuse! Exposure is going to be a very bumpy ride, but hold on and keep moving forward. This part will take a whole lot of courage. People often think that having courage is a character trait that some people are just born with, but that is not true! Create a habit of evaluating any feelings of fear, anxiety, stress, or doubt and breathe. Sometimes we can mistake excitement for fear, or risk for opportunity, or the unknown for danger. Make a plan and move forward past the fear. Practicing avoidance will cause our brains to reward us with relief, but practicing courage will result in our brains rewarding us with a sense of power. Courage is a habit and a learned behavior.

We must have witnesses to our oaths and agreements we make with each other. You had witnesses to the marriage; and therefore, you do, at some points in this process, need witnesses to the dissolution of the marriage. Therefore, invite him to come forward, with witnesses, to make amends. Do not do this alone even by phone; you need a witness. If he comes forward before witnesses with a sincere apology that is free of arrogance and speaks the truth of his actions *and* makes amends, then forgive. It still does not mean you must forget, lest you repeat the past. You can and should continue to tell your story to help others. But if he is a coward, he will not come forward. He will continue to hide, or he may have someone else come forward for him to feel you out. If he continues to hide or continues to deploy his smear campaign, then seek justice for yourself, your children, your family, and for other sisters in the community.

> But if they cease, Allah/God is Oft-forgiving, Most Merciful. And fight them on until there is no more tumult or oppression, and there prevail justice and faith in Allah; but if they cease, let there be no hostility except to those who practice oppression. (Al-Quran 2:192–193)

> Allah does not like that evil should be uttered in public except by him who has been wronged. (Quran An-Nisa 4:148)

The purpose of exposing the abuse to leaders in your religious and secular community is not to make a public scandal. A public scandal has the potential to (1) glorify the evil deeds of another, (2) be malicious gossip, (3) be slander or libel, and (4) exposure of the oppression which should be for the purpose of making public corrections without malice. When you expose this abuse, be sure to only expose the crime of abandonment and those things that are related to the emotional abuse and manipulation that led to or facilitated the abandonment.

Please know that he will try to hide the elephant in the room (his abandonment and/or abuse) by throwing a napkin over it! The narcissist is skilled at muddying the waters and gaslighting to confuse onlookers and get them focused on the napkin that he has thrown to cover his cruelty. By now, you already know this about the narcissist, so do not fall into that trap. The narcissist is very predictable once you know who you are dealing with.

Items 1–3 above are forbidden. But number 4, public correction without malice, can be accomplished by a person of authority among you. However, under the law, a public complaint can be lodged by *any person* who has suffered oppression or abuse. So lodge your complaint in writing to the religious community! You have every right! A sample public complaint can be found in the appendices. *Document the incident.* File a report to the Imams or ministers, whether they are willing to act or not. If you should have to appear in a court of law for a divorce hearing, you can also request that the Imam testify about your rights as a Muslim woman or any other religious rights. If your Imam is not brave enough to stand up, you can seek an Imam outside of your community, because he will still be considered an expert witness in the courts. The judge will not rule on these things alone; however, this information may and can be considered.

This is going to be hard because the first thought may be to hide the abuse, because too often, the victim is scrutinized. Who needs that on top of what you are already dealing with? But coming forward will prevent other sisters from going through this trauma. *If you hide the abuse, you will impede the healing process and securing your rights.*

If you are in a community where the authorities among you are not strong enough to stand up, there are some cities in the country where abandonment is more prevalent. Surprisingly, this could be a possible place to seek support. These communities are already actively fighting this type of abuse and may be able to provide referrals, representation, documents, and other forms of support.

In addition, your mental health counselor can be called as an expert witness to the psychological abuse that you and your children suffered. Be sure to bring other trusted family members or members of the religious community to witness the court proceedings. Men who inflict this type of abuse count on living in secrecy. He may even try to ask the court to remove the community members, but the courthouse is a public place, and as long as they are not testifying, they are allowed to observe any hearings. You want to expose the truth for your own protection and to record the injustice. Leave a paper trail to document the abuse. That is all you can do to protect others in the community.

So what will *you* do now? The manipulation tactics used to inflict the psychological abuse was a process that span months, if not years. Therefore, the recovery will take time. Your disposition will get better each day, and you will be yourself again, just new and improved, with an additional arsenal of protection, which is knowledge of the narcissists and their manipulation tactics. You will be prepared!

Despite the distress that you have suffered, you must be grateful that you have learned a great deal from your hardship. You have learned how to spot the covert and open narcissist and how to determine if you are being groomed for narcissistic abuse and/or abandonment. You have learned that the low quality of life and lack of emotional and spiritual fulfillment is not something that you want in your life. You have learned that you are indeed a survivor, and you can overcome all obstacles with love of yourself, faith, and perseverance.

Just like any other form of abuse or injury, once you have recovered, you will likely have scars. But these are battle scars of triumph, not scars of defeat. When you remember where those scars came from, you won't repeat your mistakes. You will go into a subsequent courtship better informed and clear on what red flags are. You will know how to say no at any stage, even after the engagement, even coming down the aisle; it is never too late! You will be more adamant about your own mental, spiritual, and emotional safety, and you will be a beacon of light for those who find themselves lost in this web.

Do not become a proponent against marriage. Instead, be an informative ear on how to avoid your own mistakes. If you do not, then all the pain, anguish, and injustice you have suffered will have been for naught. Let your struggle mean a better way of life for you as well as the sisters that you can positively inform that the institution of marriage is a blessing!

> Oh humanity! Be mindful of your Lord who created you from a single soul, and from it He created its mate, and through both He spread countless men and women. And be mindful of Allah (God)—in Whose Name you appeal to one another—and honor family ties. Surely Allah is ever Watchful over you. (Quran 4:1)

You may be weary thinking about starting over. You are not starting over; you are starting again, which takes courage. It is the courage to recognize that you are worthy of the life Allah has intended for you. This experience, as horrible as it was, has left you empowered with knowledge, wisdom, and understanding that the human spirit is still worthy of your trust. Good men are still worthy of your trust.

Decide to live your best life now as God has cleared a path for you by removing people and things from your life that mean you no good. The next time around, you will know how to determine that you have found a man who wants to be a husband and not a man who just wants to possess and/or showcase a wife to build his counterfeit persona. Please know that Allah can see around corners, beyond curtains, and behind masks. He has saved you from a worse fate that could have been inflicted by the narcissist, and you have not been harmed beyond repair! Seek knowledge from all available sources. Allah has a plan for us, and the best life has to offer is a part of that plan. Anyone can choose to live outside of that plan, and many times in life, we will get sidetracked, manipulated, or off course due to lack of understanding. But when we avail ourselves to His supreme knowledge, we can get back on His path and live in His plan and under His protection. This, applying His supreme knowledge to how we live our lives, is what leads to wisdom.

You must believe in yourself and your ability to grow from this experience. When life gives you lemons…write a book! Yes! Do just that. It doesn't mean you must have all the answers. You can write about your experiences and about your journey. Although you may not know what *to do*, you can surely share with others what *not to do*! There is wisdom in that as well.

Be grateful! We must be grateful even in times of struggle. We must thank Allah that (1) it wasn't worse, because things can always be worse; (2) that we learned patience and perseverance; (3) that we can still count some blessings in our lives; and (4) that, at least, it was not our faith that was tested!

Once again, buckle up, sisters! It's going to be a bumpy ride, but just be courageous! The Creator will forever be with those who are oppressed, so *never* lose faith in Him. In the darkest of tunnels, I still knew that Allah was with me. I hope and pray this clarity for you as well. Sometimes we learn and grow in prosperity, but often, the most extraordinary growth will come in times of hardship, so when you are in the curve of a dark tunnel and cannot see the light, just keep moving forward. Keep praying, keep expecting happiness, keep believing in the future that was intended for you to have. Keep keepin' on, as the old folks say. Expect happiness because you deserve to be happy, and you have nothing to fear! Expect to reach your fullest potential in this life! Expect more, and you will receive more.

No matter how dark it seems, you must hold on to the rope of Allah! Do *not* let go! As they say, "When you get to the end of your rope, tie a knot and *hang on!*"

On a sunny Saturday in October 2021, my son and I suffered a premeditated abandonment on the infamous wedding anniversary vacation in Myrtle Beach. We returned home on Sunday driving through a raging storm to find that my then husband had packed up and left the home while we were sleeping two states away. I started a new job on Monday in despair; the in-home care of my dad transitioned to hospice care, and he passed six weeks later. It seemed everywhere I turned, there was darkness. Fast-forward to October

2022. The fight for my rights as a Muslim woman and wife is won. I returned to Myrtle Beach to a wonderful vacation, and this time, going back home to a new job with less stress and more pay. Things may not always move so quickly, but you must stay the course because Allah has a restoration planned for you! Do not get sidetracked or derailed from your goal. Restoration is not full recovery, but it's a start. I attribute this restoration to belief in Allah, support of family and friends, and a willingness to speak out in hopes of helping others. You must speak out and rid yourself of the anguish. Do not carry anguish around, or it will become a weight and a cancer. You will get stronger each day that you survive the narcissistic tornado that blew through your life. Each hour, day, month, and year that you do not give up will make a difference.

I know that you can do this because I am writing the last words of this book from Myrtle Beach, South Carolina! The fact that I am ending this story right where it began (the place of the abandonment) cannot pass without mention. The formal complaint of abandonment and desertion lodged to the Muslim community grew into an invite to write a seven-week column in the *Muslim Journal*. Then it became this book that is ironically being completed in the place that was meant to be used as a weapon against me. Here, I sit eleven months and two weeks later in the place I vowed that I would never return to again because the thought was so traumatic. I was going to Myrtle Beach before I met him, and I should continue to go afterward.

So my sister/friend Arlandria and I packed up our kids and her nephew, and we met in Myrtle Beach. The timing, a week before that wedding anniversary trip and the completion of this book, was quite by accident or maybe divinely guided. The location was because it was a good halfway place to meet up for fun and sun before summer comes to an end. She drove from Georgia, and I drove from Virginia. We pulled up to the beach house at the exact same time, a great start to a great weekend. And guess what? Lo and behold, the sun is still shining in Myrtle Beach, the sand is still warm between our toes, the crab legs are still sweet, and the go-carts still bring squeals of laughter, big smiles, and lots of fun! Life brings you full circle to face the past, and Allah gives you the strength to do it fearlessly!

I know you can do it because I am an ordinary sister who was dealt an extraordinarily nasty hand. Nevertheless, I knew that Allah's promise is true, and after *every* hardship, He will bring us ease. Allah's promise is true that every weapon used against His believers will fail. Allah's promise is true that you must expose abuse and oppression by speaking out because a lie will *never* defeat the *truth*! Allah will always protect the believers and expose the hypocrites, and if you wait, the hypocrites will expose themselves! Speak out, sisters, because it will help you heal and it will help countless others to heal as well. You can overcome some extraordinary obstacles and heal just by speaking out. Please accept, access, speak out, fight for your rights, and most of all, pray. This recipe will allow you to bloom wherever you are planted! Can we have a hashtag for that too? #BloomWhereYouArePlanted

Full Case Studies from Women Who Share True Accounts Referenced in This Book

Please read the following full case studies/interviews shared by these women specifically for the purpose of this book. Learn about their hardship, healing, and triumph to prepare and strengthen yourself for the journey to come. I applaud these women for daring to be heard. I thank them from the bottom of my heart for entrusting me with their personal lives. I know the process of reliving the trauma was extremely hard for them, but they hung in there with me because they were dedicated to helping others and they want for their sisters what they want for themselves. These women are superheroes!

I hope and pray that you will gain strength from this book and will live a life full of love, light, and purpose. Survival is just a first step to thriving, so I pray that this work will give you strength and courage and allow you to speak out and be heard. I pray that it has given a voice to the voiceless. I pray that if you have suffered, that life will be good for you again and that you will thrive again! Mashallah, God has already willed it!

CASE STUDY NO. 1

Nia—The Abandoning Fiancé

Demographics

Age: 39
Race/Ethnicity: Black Caribbean
Occupation: Educator
Religion: Islam
Number of His Previous Marriages and/or Engagements: 4 confirmed marriages prior and several broken engagements

Red Flags

Red flag no. 1—He insists he is ready for marriage or commitment immediately
Red flag no. 4—He always says the right thing and tries a bit too hard

Red flag no. 5—He blames his ex-wife for the entire demise of the
    marriage
Red flag no. 8—He violates boundaries
Red flag no. 9—Additional red flags realized after the fact

In the process of an individual working toward securing the trust and love from a potential victim in the narcissistic dynamic, the words the perpetrator uses are often deceptive. The perpetrator knows the exact words to say and practices to use that will cause the victim to trust him. The perpetrator also knows what actions will garner the best results for the devastation of the target.

The following red flags were discovered that were put in use in the victimization of Case Study No. 1 participant. Although Case Study No. 1 did not become entangled with marriage with the perpetrator, there is still much hurt and harm done to the victim because of the practices employed during the brief relationship of betrayal.

The first day I met him, he called me a unicorn. He said that I was special and rare. In my wakil's presence, he told me that I was a breath of fresh air.

During our second conversation, he referred to me as beloved and said that he was my future intended husband. I was a bit concerned about him calling me beloved so quickly; he did not know me well enough to be using terms of endearment so early. It's as though he was forcing me further into a relationship we weren't even in yet.

I asked a couple of my friends if his calling me beloved after meeting me one time wasn't strange. Some said that old-school men have a tendency to talk to women that way. I ended up shrugging it off.

I thought he was the perfect man because he wanted to support and extend my dreams beyond what I had imagined and shared with him. When I told him I was a certified fitness trainer, he quickly responded that he was already working out the details in his head about how he would help me establish a business. He spoke of opening a fitness studio for me to run and even said we could have a juice bar. It was music to my ears to hear this! I was tired of coming across men who wanted to build their success off the backs of women. This man was offering me the world at my feet.

I am a very active, adventurous person. Guys are typically threatened by this; they usually express concern that I couldn't possibly be an attentive wife if I want to lead such a busy life. My intended had no problem with the activities I engaged in. He claimed to be just as adventurous and looked forward to us doing many things together. He might very well have been an adventurous, fun-loving husband. I'll never know. He chose to abandon me the day after proposing without any explanation.

He wanted to purchase a home for me and described what it would look like in great detail.

When I shared with him how deeply hurt I was that my children's father refused to play an active role in their lives, he talked about being a good father figure to my children.

He blamed his ex-wife for their divorce, claiming that she did not want to be in polygyny. He said he was a good husband to his ex-wife and had even paid for her schooling after they divorced. He wanted to make sure she was able to take care of herself and the children he had with her. After he ghosted me, I was able to speak with his ex-wife. She did not have an issue with him practicing polygyny; she was tired of the year of abuse she had suffered at his hand.

Neither had he paid for her schooling. He apparently said that to my wakil to make himself look kindhearted, generous, and honorable—qualities I had often prayed for in a partner. I was thrilled to learn that he possessed them and that I was going to be a wife to such a wonderful man. Little did I know that it was all a facade to reel me into his web. He was a gentleman up until the night he asked me to marry him. My wakil was in another room. After my intended used the bathroom, he came from behind and playfully tickled me, then rubbed his left shoulder against my right shoulder. He was well aware that no physical contact is allowed between a man and a woman unless they are married. I was surprised by what he did but did not object because it was very brief and unexpected. Additionally, I was attracted to him.

That played a factor in me not correcting his behavior.

After he ghosted me, I discovered that he had done the same thing to several other women. I spoke to women whose friends had sat with my former intended. It was revealed that he would ask the women to marry him, tell them to start looking for apartments for them to move into, then abruptly stopped communicating with them and ignored them if he saw them in public. I was also informed by one of his former wives and a prominent wakil in the community that he was married too many times to count. The marriages always ended badly; many of the marriages lasted less than a year. Had I known this, I may not have given him the time of day. Too many marriages is an indication that an individual may have quite a lot of baggage and some reform to do on himself.

Whenever I sat with my former intended, he was so attentive; we had such great conversations. He seemed to adore me and gave me beautiful compliments. However, after sit-downs, he took a long time to get back to my wakil about our next sit-down. This caused me a great deal of anxiety. I could not understand how he could be so into me when we sat, but it would take my wakil reaching out to him after a couple of weeks to inquire about when we would sit again.

At some point, we were in a group chat with my wakil. My former intended took four to five days to respond to messages I sent to him. Again, I couldn't understand how he professed to be so interested in me and wouldn't make time to respond, even briefly, to my texts. Mind you, the group chat was his idea. He wanted to be able to check in with me every day to see how I was doing.

My heart and mind did not feel right about the huge delays in his responses to my wakil about when we would meet again, nor concerning his delayed responses to my texts. I firmly believe that people make time for what's important to them.

I began to question if he was playing games with me. I was assured by my wakil that things were progressing as they should. He assured me that my intended was a very busy man based on the nature of the business he managed, which was in mental health. Still, I had my doubts.

CASE STUDY NO. 2

Monica—The Family Friend

Demographics

Age: 59
Race/Ethnicity: African American
Occupation: Chief of staff in federal government
Religion: Christian
Number of Previous Marriages for Him: 2

Red Flags

Red flag no. 1—Immediate readiness for marriage
Red flag no. 2—Excessive information requested or given
Red flag no. 3—Rejection of sit-downs
Red flag no. 4—Always saying the right things and trying a bit too
hard
Red flag no. 5—The blame game

Red flag no. 6—Negative comments about family
Red flag no. 7—Does not want a written marriage contract or legal
marriage license
Red flag no. 8—He violates boundaries and is inconsistent
Red flag no. 9—Additional red flags

Familiarity Is Not Always Good

When one is unknowingly entering into a narcissistic dynamic to include someone with whom you may have had a relationship with before, what you may have previously known about a person can be completely different to what is actually true about that person in the narcissistic space.

In Case Study No. 2, the participants had known each other for many years. But that knowledge did not dig deep enough into the truth behind the would-be perpetrator as he victimizes his next target.

Instances of Demeaning or Ghosting; Instances of His Friends, Flying Monkeys, Hovering Over and Bringing Messages to Reel You Back into the Relationship

He routinely went silent. One time, he didn't call me for two weeks. Then there was the CIAA basketball tournament event during which he was out and about with an ex-girlfriend. Someone always came about that was more interesting. I broke off the relationship; he begged me to take him back. I told him that this was the last time, or we would be done for good.

Eight months later, he went silent again. This time, I ended the relationship. At this point, I lost all respect for him. I did not accept any more apologies. Really, I was waiting for something big to happen so it could be over. I needed something that would make it too hard for me to take him back. I was finally done.

Even then, though, he had one of his friends call and tell me that he was coming to town and really wanted to see me. When I said no, his friend was shocked and couldn't believe it! I was finally done.

A week later, he texted me and said, "I am going to be in town. I would love for you to join me." I finally ignored his every attempt to get my attention. He then asked me to join him for Valentine's Day. When I was not receptive and was finally out of his reach, he began showering me with attention, again, because he always wants to win. Unfortunately, he had a stroke, but this did not prevent him from trying to contact me once again.

At his father's funeral, he asked one of my friends if I was coming. He was still making attempts to see me. There were other opportunities. He was still trying to reach out to me through friends. If I knew he was going to be somewhere I would potentially be, I made sure to not be there. He had rekindled things with his wife but continued to pursue me. I continued to be unavailable.

Sometimes he tried to make me look bad for his advantage. He told others that I was melodramatic and a drama queen.

Negative Mental, Physical, Spiritual, or Financial Effects of This Abuse

There were constant disappointments and lies during our relationship. There were also constant promises to divorce his wife. He would actually go to divorce court at least once or twice a year!

At the beginning of our relationship, he had called my uncle to ask for permission to marry me.

My uncle said, "Aren't you married?"

He said, "No. We are in divorce court."

My uncle told him that if/when the divorce became final, then yes, he could have his blessing to pursue me. But he pursued me anyway. This went on for years with him filing for divorce at least seven times during the time we were together.

After one of the divorce filings, he suggested that we get a house together, saying it (his marriage) was finally over. He said for me to get the loan, and he would pay the down payment and buy things for the house. We went house hunting. We found a house, and he sent me the money for the down payment. I packed up my home; I had scheduled the movers. It was three days before moving day, and we went shopping for furniture.

He got a phone call. It was his *supposed* soon-to-be ex-wife. I was confused. When I questioned him, he went into a tirade and said we didn't need to do this and that it was my fault for starting the argument. Now we wouldn't be moving into the house that I already had the loan for, the movers, etc. He asked for the money back! I refused. He said if I didn't return the money, we could not be anything in the future. I moved into the house alone. He was supposed to pay half the mortgage; now it was a financial struggle. I finally sold the house after living there for almost two years.

Although my hair began to thin out from the stress, I never had any other physical illness. I experienced depression for a few months when he went back to his wife that he had supposedly been getting a divorce from.

To this day, it has been three years, though I still have trauma and anxiety when I think about all that I went through and the deception and manipulation I was subjected to.

Effects of Post-Traumatic Stress Syndrome

I continue to experience recurring dreams now and then. I feel like I was in a war. It had been three years, and his name or seeing certain things still evokes trauma. His friends, family, and colleagues had no idea of what he was capable of. It was later discovered that he was using his job's expense account to fund his love-bombing of me; he was a high-level salesperson for an international hotel chain.

Advice to Other Women Seeking Marriage

If you meet someone who says they are getting a divorce or in divorce court and they have not been happy for years, just say "When you get a divorce, *if* I am still free, call me. But until that time, I am not available" and move on.

Look for signs that you are either really important to the person or that you are just a trophy or arm candy.

His friend told me one time, "What do you think of the situation of the dog on the sand hill? You know, the dog will bark at

142

anyone coming on the sand hill although he does not want to be on the sand hill either."

Advice to Someone Abandoned in a Relationship

Don't go back! I don't know how to tell you to get through it. It's so traumatic that you will only get through it by the grace of God! It is so traumatic to you, but to them, it's fun and games.

He will say that you are being dramatic, that in the end, it is all your fault. He will give you his word. In reality, though, don't even believe that! He will say whatever he has to say to get whatever he wants.

Additional Thoughts and Situations

He was addicted to sex. He had told me about his previous wife saying he must go to counseling for this. He said she was crazy, but I knew that this was an addiction for him. No matter what you do for them, they will not overcome this addiction. There is *nothing* you can do to help this.

*****

The following red flags were observed after the fact as Case Study No. 2 was victimized:

He said that he loved me and wanted to spend the rest of his life with me. Since we had known each other for over forty-five years, grown up in the same city, and dated when we were in our twenties, I didn't think too much about it.

He often told me I was his soul mate and was very eager to spend time with my family. He even called my uncle and asked him if he could marry me.

Because we had known each other for such a long time and kept in contact, I did not find myself giving him too much information or him requesting too much information from me. I knew his family and was able to keep up with him over the years through them and vice versa.

He never wanted to have any discussions about anything serious. At the suggestion, he would shut down, giving the excuse that he talked for a living. He explained that he didn't want to have to do all this talking in his relationship.

I found that he was mimicking my thoughts, hopes, and dreams after I shared certain things with him. I also discovered that bonds were beginning to exist when it was just a little too soon in the relationship.

In the first few months, he confessed his love for me. After that, he rarely told me he loved me.

He always seemed to be very well rehearsed when we were around family and friends. But he was a different person to me than the one he presented to his family, friends, and colleagues.

When we rekindled our relationship, he admitted to me that he was working on getting a divorce. Although he never blamed any of his ex-wives for the demise of their relationships, he did share that they stopped getting along because his first wife and current wife started taking him for granted. He always shared with me what they did wrong but never said what role he played in the ending of the relationships. However, in the very beginning of our relationship, I surmised that he could be a very difficult person to get along with.

His family thought very highly of him and would cover for him in his deceptions. To them, he walked on water.

I did not experience him making negative comments about his family because we had known each other all our lives. I called his dad every Sunday.

As we got closer in the beginning, he first told me that he wanted to get married as soon as his divorce was final. As time progressed, though, he suggested that we just live together when his divorce was finalized. He filed for divorce from his current wife five times in the seven years we were together. He is still married to her until this day.

He constantly canceled or backed out of commitments. It was one disappointment after another. I never felt like I mattered or that my feelings were important. Even though he would ask me what I wanted for dinner, he always found reasons why my choice wasn't going to work for him.

He always reminded me that he was a strong man. He always said that strong men don't let women control them.

Safia—The Honeymoon of Horrors

Demographics

Age: 38
Race/Ethnicity: African American
Occupation: Behavioral therapist / educator
Religion: Islam
Number of Previous Marriages for Him: 1

Red Flags

Red flag no. 1—Immediate readiness for marriage
Red flag no. 2—Excessive information requested or given

Red flag no. 4—Always saying the right things and trying a bit too
  hard
Red flag no. 5—The blame game
Red flag no. 6—Negative comments about family
Red flag no. 7—Does not want a written marriage contract or legal
  marriage license
Red flag no. 8—He violates boundaries and is inconsistent
Red flag no. 9—Additional red flags

Narcissism hurts. It destroys…and not just the victim. Whether
the perpetrator knows it or not or acknowledges it or not, the narcissism they carry is something that will eventually be like a cancer and
will cause them to never be who they were created to be because of
the negative energy of the narcissistic abuse.

In Case Study No. 3, everything was done very quickly—the
beginning, the middle, and the ending. But there is a happy ending…just not with the narcissist.

From Subject Safia

I recognized all the signs in my partner.

Stage 1. To me, love-bombing looked like he was just extremely
interested in me. There was a lot of mirroring. The first time he met
me, he got in touch with me through my social media. He studied
me. Once he found out I had a podcast, he watched every single
podcast, which was cool to me. That was actually a pull for me. The
average man I was courting was like, "That's great that you have a
podcast." They would tune in for support, but the level of study my
ex utilized in love-bombing me was exceptional. He watched every
podcast multiple times.

In retrospect, I now know that he was mirroring me. At the
time, I was not consciously aware of this. He was good on the topics
I was good on. He raised issues and was passionate about the things I
had going on my podcast. He would immediately see what he could
add value to with the podcast. He then created my logo and created
products; I still use those things to this day. He did these things very

early on in our attachment, like in the first one to two weeks. He made really big, huge, grand gestures. He purchased big major items for my platform.

He made sure he was in contact with me every day, all day. There was an excessive amount of phone calls, an excessive amount of face time, an excessive amount of texts. Not an hour went by without there being contact between us. I just thought that this was someone who was extremely interested in me. But it was very, very excessive.

At a certain point, I remember feeling overwhelmed. I asked him to give me time because I needed to focus on my work. He was really paranoid with my request. He was afraid of my taking time away from him. He tried to offer support and help and things like that. He wanted to make sure that the contact kept going.

The love-bombing phase was very intense. He made grandiose gestures with really, really large expensive purchases: Bocce sunglasses, purses, and all kinds of things. He made very, very huge gestures. Again, though, the main thing was the contact. He made sure that the contact was constant.

Stage 2. Demeaning and spirit-breaking was definitely present in our attachment. It happened little by little and was very subtle. One of his main goals was to get to the wedding.

We had signed a contract and a premarital agreement earlier before the big wedding. But he wanted a very grandiose, over-the-top wedding. It was really important for him to maintain that control until that point. I recall one of the early signs he gave to me when he was beginning to go into the breakdown stage. We had a great weekend here, we spent a lot of time together, and we were super close. Everything was fine. When he got on the plane, though, he immediately withdrew.

He acted strange. He said he was going through some things; he just withdrew.

I was very confused. At the time, we were about four or five months into the relationship. Leading up to this point, he had called me on the hour, every hour; he never let an hour go by without contact. He went from that to withdrawing completely, to not calling at all. I would call; I would text. He wouldn't answer. Or he would act super busy and get off the phone quickly if he did answer. That was the first time.

I began to panic. I did not know what was wrong. Of course, I went and tried to figure it all out.

He would make up excuses, saying he was going through some things. That was the first sign of the drop from the high to the extreme low. It caused me a lot of anxiety and confusion. And then he brought it right back around to love-bombing maybe about a week later. That was the first time.

From there, he would do very little subtle things in the break-down stage. He made subtle comments. He gave a lot of compliments in love-bombing, then his compliments abruptly stopped. He no longer complimented my appearance; he no longer made compliments about being lucky and things like that. That started happening slowly but surely.

But the moment after the wedding, when we were starting on the actual honeymoon, he went into full-fledged demeaning mode. He was criticizing; he was putting me down. Our honeymoon was actually very traumatic. He left me alone at a place because he was mad. He did the most abrupt, abrasive things out of the blue on the honeymoon. His demeaning and breakdown started right after that wedding. From that point on, it was hell.

Stage 3. Abandonment/discard happened again after the wedding. A week after we got back from the honeymoon, he made up a story about being so stressed from work and some other things. He immediately left. He abandoned me and went back to his home. He either planned this for him to move his stuff here. He literally abandoned me. He didn't come back to our home until maybe about four months later. I would go up and visit him, but he did not come back to our home during those four months.

The abandonment phase, at the time, I didn't see it as abandonment because he made tons and tons of excuses. I would go up to see him and try to figure things out because he claimed he was working and taking care of business. He was never really working. He never paid one bill after the wedding or after the honeymoon.

And so a slow kind of abandonment happened. He literally never returned. When he did come back, I threatened to leave. He came back for a week. While he was there, he created all this chaos and confusion. There was a big argument, and that was his excuse to leave. He always tried to manipulate the situation and make it seem like I started the argument so he would have an excuse to leave. The abandonment, though, literally started right after the wedding.

*****

The following red flags were observed after the fact as Case Study No. 3 was victimized:

He insisted he was ready for marriage or commitment immediately. That was pretty apparent. He went right into that right away. He started sending pictures of houses for us to consider and wedding venues from day 2 or day 3.

He did offer up some information to me. He was actually pretty transparent about certain things, I guess you could say. But everything had a very serious manipulative spin on it. A lot of it was cold-blooded lies and stuff he would say about his exes.

He did a lot of mirroring at the beginning. He killed, and when I say he killed, I mean he killed some dough to get to that wedding, that really over-the-top, grandiose wedding. He sacrificed everything to get there.

There was a big, huge thing going on in his life. Come to find out, the ex was the one he was definitely still sleeping with, in a relationship with. I couldn't figure out why she was losing her mind. She was out of her mind, crazy. He made her sound like she was crazy and just a deranged woman. Otherwise, she was just another victim of narcissistic abuse.

Yes, there were definitely negative comments about his family. He was always the victim, he was the abused child, and he was the abandoned kid. Nobody ever loved him. Nobody gave him anything. That was always his story.

The only time he really had an issue was when it came time for the marriage contract to be written. Although he eventually signed it, he did have an issue with it. He made a big deal about doing a legal civil license and things like that. After the wedding, though, he said nothing more about it.

He completely violated every single boundary I had established all the time. I had a lot of boundaries, especially when it came to other women, my privacy, and even just physical boundaries. He violated each and every one of them all the time. He had a huge issue with boundaries.

He did not have a problem with showing me off at his masjid. He grabbed me and proudly swung me around the community, showed me off to everybody who was looking. That was a big part of his draw to me; I think he thought I was good arm candy.

Additional Red Flags

1. My ex was an overt narcissist. There were definitely signs that were overlooked:

    - History of aggression
    - History of violence
    - Often speaking about violence
    - Often speaking about his past, his past crime often

    These were red flags really early on. I wasn't bothered by any of it until a lot of family members started talking about these things. I went to my coach and said, "You know, this person is talking about his past crime life, and this is troubling to me." A lot of people talked me out of my conflicting thoughts. They said such things as, "You know, he probably needs a place to vent," "You know, he probably never had someone listen to him," and things like that. But that was a red flag. I was not really paying attention to the things that he did. I didn't really listen to the things that he said. The things he said were his true lifestyle. That was the lifestyle he really lived. When it was all exposed, he was still in the life of crime, he was still into drugs, he was still engaged in sexual relationships, and he was still engaged in all those things, even though he talked about those things as if they were in the past. Because of the way he presented his life, I also treated those things as if they were in the past. But he talked about it so much; that was a red flag.

2. Another thing is social media. There is a red flag in social media when, as a man, you have a ridiculous amount of random unknown female friends, and most of these women you didn't know. The red flag for me was that we had so many mutual friends that were mostly females.

   None of them personally knew him. Additionally, he had been in so many different people's inboxes. I didn't find this out until later. But again, the red flag was not just the social media. It was just the majority were women. I remember that coming up earlier on.

   Immediately he responded, "Okay, no problem. I will unfollow them. You know, that's really nothing. You know, I see music and I just stop." He had those kinds of excuses.

   After the wedding, and when we were in the big part of abandonment and the demeaning stage, all of a sudden, all these social media women were so important to him. He had to maintain his women friends; it just became such a thing. Before, he made it seem like just so matter-of-fact that he didn't know how they ended up on his FB page. "I didn't even know. I just accept everybody." He had all these excuses. He was in his full-fledged manipulation, kind of faithfulness manipulation.

   These women were very present. All of a sudden, these were his friends. They were people he had to stay in contact with.

3. Another huge red flag is the phone. How the narcissistic abuser treats his phone really matters.

   One of the things I can tell you is that, in the beginning, he never paid too much attention to his phone. The phone wasn't too visible in the earlier occasions when we were together. Once the relationship got into play, though, once he had me hooked, once he had me there, he always had a phone in his hand.

He would go into the bathroom for an hour, two hours, with the phone. He would make it seem like he was using the bathroom. He was in the bathroom, on the phone, on dating apps and talking to other supplies. He would keep his phone under his belly.

He also had two phones. He eventually acquired a second phone number in the relationship with me. Another red flag, and that's a common narcissistic trait. They have different multiple numbers and multiple social media accounts.

He kept a social media account for his old school's name; he had a social media account for his new school name. That's also a red flag. Using multiple types of identities is also an indicator that they have multiple things going on. The phone and what they do with their phones is the biggest red flag.

I'm in a very healthy relationship now. My partner gladly hands his phone to me if I ask. He gladly leaves his phone unlocked around.

CASE STUDY NO. 4

Tara—A Very Slippery Slope

Demographics

Age: 50
Race/Ethnicity: Caucasian
Occupation: Marketing consultant
Religion: Christian

Red Flags

Red flag no. 1—Immediate readiness for marriage
Red flag no. 2—Excessive information requested or given
Red flag no. 3—Rejection of sit-downs
Red flag no. 4—Always saying the right things and trying a bit too hard
Red flag no. 5—The blame game
Red flag no. 6—Negative comments about family

Red flag no. 7—Does not want a written marriage contract or legal
    marriage license
Red flag no. 8—He violates boundaries and is inconsistent
Red flag no. 9—Additional red flags

This study is a little lengthier than the previous studies because
of the information gained from the participant as well as an additional perpetrator. Not only will we see the red flags subject Tara
experienced but we will also answer more personalized questions
from the experience.

We will begin with and address the three segments of the abusive cycle: beginning, middle, end. Then we will proceed with the red
flags this participant experienced.

The Beginning

I experienced abandonment when my ex very unexpectedly
asked me for a divorce after I confronted him about why he was
spending so much time with a female coworker. We were already on
a slippery slope down the road of pornography and then, eventually,
a swinging lifestyle in which we would have other couples over just
for sex. Toward the end, my ex would find single men and send me
over to their places to have sex with them and send the video back to
him. When we started this lifestyle, he promised me that at any time,
either of us could say stop and we would stop. There were many
times I asked to stop; he never did. This also showed up with him
being very controlling over my eating and working out, my dress,
hairstyles, etc.

The manipulation was a slow walk. What I mean by that is, it
started with just going to the local porn store and looking at magazines. Then it was getting some movies. The next thing I know, we
owned a huge library of pornography. Then he posed the conversation of "What would it be like to actually have someone else with
us?" Then he signed us up on a swinger's website. The progression
happened over about a nine-year period of time. He would always tell

me if I was ever uncomfortable, all I had to do was say no. However, I said no many times, and he never stopped.

There were several things that caused me to continue down the path; all of them point back to a place of being uneducated about relationships, people, and dating. I was also functioning from a very naive ideal of marriage and what that covenant relationship really means. To add into the mix, I didn't have a very secure feeling of self or the power I had to choose; I moved forward with a "hope" that everything would be okay.

I didn't know I actually had a choice in the relationship before we got married. There were many things that didn't feel good about the relationship; some that actually scared me. But I had it in my mind that I needed to get married, and since he was the first one I met, he was supposed to be my husband.

I didn't believe I could actually make it on my own, and I didn't know how else I would meet someone (low self-esteem).

I didn't understand one person's inability to "change" anyone else. I had a feeling in me that if I just loved him enough, I could change whatever didn't feel right and everything would work out.

He began spending a lot of time with a female from his work. He claimed he was helping her study. He would leave my daughter and me several nights a week and at least once on the weekends to be with her. Although he said that nothing physical ever happened between them, he left us for her even after I asked him to stay multiple times. The final split happened when seemingly out of nowhere, he said he wanted a divorce.

I had no idea that this was coming. I was trying my hardest to do whatever I could for my husband. I knew about the other woman and was fairly accommodating to his request to go and study with her. I felt like he had his cake and was eating it too, so why would he *ever* ask for a divorce?

Emotional, Mental, Physical, and Financial Tolls of Abandonment and Desertion of You, Your Children, Your Family

My self-worth diminished, too, next to nothing. I was very anxious and afraid that he would come back and physically hurt me. I was prescribed antidepressants to help me get through the divorce proceedings and the first months away from him.

My daughter was almost four when we divorced. Now at the age of twenty, she is currently coming to grips with her dad's behavior. We shared fifty-fifty custody. As a result, she experienced years of his manipulation. I tried my best to never speak poorly of him to her. Due to his treatment, she is currently working on her tendency to be a people pleaser.

My daughter and I have discovered that we no longer have a preference in certain situations in life after what we experienced. When we are asked "What would you like for dinner?" we have found that we never have an answer. During my marriage, my ex would ask the same question. If I responded, "Oh, chipotle sounds good," he would then reply, "Oh, I don't want that. I want _____." It came down to me trying to guess what he wanted instead of me having a preference. In this way, it felt as though I was getting my way. In actuality, it stripped me of part of who I am. My daughter finds herself doing the same.

Just before our separation, we sold our home with the intention of downsizing. We did this because he wanted to change jobs for the second time, taking huge pay cuts with each new position. We ended up purchasing a home that cost us more than the house we had just sold. After being in our new house for about two weeks, things with us finally ended. We had to short sell the house and lost all the equity we had accumulated from our previous house. During our relationship, one of the ways he dealt with his bad moods or insecurities was shopping. When we split, we were upside down in both cars and our house. We had credit card debt, a debt to my parents, and no savings.

Response from Family and Others

Not only was he manipulative toward my daughter and me but he was also very manipulative toward his parents. His relationship with them was severely damaged. While we were still married, his parents had moved out of state to get away from his verbal and emotional abuse. When they found out we were divorcing, they moved back to help with his parenting time with our daughter.

Eventually, his parents had had enough of his manipulation and abusive treatment; they legally disowned him. They reached out to me so they could have a relationship with their granddaughter. We have built a healthy friendship, and he has no further connection with his parents.

Did You Have Any Type of Warning—Red Flags in the Beginning?

I had a warning that he had a bad temper within the first few weeks of our relationship. He demonstrated road rage that really scared me. I managed to dismiss his actions.

Another warning came when my friend from college invited me to visit her in Santa Fe. By this time, my ex and I had been dating for a few months. He made a big deal about me going to Santa Fe alone. He accused me in advance of finding someone else when I went down there.

What Happened Leading Up to the Abandonment?

- A week before he asked for the divorce, I was extremely depressed. We had gotten into a fight when I addressed him about kissing this other woman good night outside our new home after a get-together with his coworkers. It was much more than a friendly kiss. He told me I was making a bigger deal out of it than it was. He also used the excuse that since I was going over and sleeping with other men, why was I so bent out of shape about him being with her? Even though my being with other men was his idea. He stormed off and went to bed.

I stayed downstairs in the kitchen, seriously contemplating suicide. I even had a knife to my wrist. I believe God spoke to me to put the knife down. I obeyed. Scared, I went up to tell him what had just happened. I told him I needed him to hold me. He replied, "You selfish b———. I can't believe you would even think of killing yourself. What would Shae [our daughter] and I do? I can't even look at you right now, let alone touch you!"

First Feelings/Emotions Experienced after Realization of Abandonment

When my ex asked for the divorce, I first felt hurt and shock. Then quickly, an unexplained power came over me. I was glad to have a release out of the relationship. It was like an escape hatch from the abuse was opened. Then, though, there were feelings of fear and dread of how he might retaliate against me when I actually did leave him.

Your Children's Experience

Fortunately, my daughter was so young she didn't really know what was happening.

First Response of Your Family and Those in Religious or Social Circles

My parents were not very supportive, mainly because they didn't like my ex from the beginning. They saw some of the abuse that was happening. They didn't realize the extent, though, of the abuse that was going on.

My sister actually called me the night he asked for the divorce. She was very supportive in helping me get all our things that I needed out of the house. These things included clothing for my daughter and me, bank statements, investment information, the computer, etc.

Symptoms of Grief and When It Set In

I experienced many of the symptoms of grief, such as denial, anger, bargaining, depression, and acceptance. I second-guessed myself many times during the experience. During our years of coparenting, I also longed for his respect. I wanted him to honor me, my decision-making, and my parenting. I never received that honor.

Concerning our relationship, I wondered, *Can it get better?* And I would even ask myself, *Was it really that bad?* Ultimately, though, I came to the conclusion that I was had to have gotten out.

Once I began the divorce process, he asked to go to counseling. He was a police officer. He set up an appointment with the counselors used by the PD. We went to one session. The counselor asked me if I had communicated with him to not see this other woman. To me, it felt as though the counselor was part of the manipulation. I was so angry I walked out.

The Middle

Advice to Other Women about Your Experience

If you see any signs of anger, control, or manipulation to keep you from your family or friends, especially at the beginning of the relationship, *leave*!

Some Telltale Signs That a Person Is Being Groomed for Abandonment

- Demanding all your time and attention.
- Putting boundaries around when you can be with your friends and family.
- Complaining about you spending too much time at work.
- Also, be cognizant and ready to leave the relationship if he keeps nagging, pushing, or just plain ignores your boundaries. If he can't respect your *no* at the beginning, it is not something he will learn to do over time.

Questions to Ask before Marriage You Regret Not Asking

Ask about any mental diagnosis. I found out long after the divorce that my ex was diagnosed with borderline personality disorder when he was sixteen. It might be an awkward question or discussion. However, if I had known, I hope I would have made a different decision.

Ask questions about ex-spouse, if any, and previous marriage prior to committing to marriage. I would suggest having an in-depth conversation about why his previous relationship failed. If he states that everything was the ex's fault and takes no responsibility for his actions, this is a huge flag.

If he hasn't taken any time to heal from a previous relationship/marriage, step away.

Are There Things You Could Have Spotted but Missed?

The way he treated his mother, he said he loved her, but he did not respect her. His joking with her was mean. He complained about her behind her back and used her.

He had a short fuse and got upset when things didn't go his way.

He demonstrated road rage several times. He would yell at other drivers for being stupid and not knowing how to drive. He would get frustrated and speed excessively, weaving in and out of traffic. When I called him on it, he always excused his actions with, "Don't worry. I know how to drive."

He was rude to most waitstaff.

There was always an inconsistency in what was okay. For example, I could be driving down a road where the speed limit is forty-five and I'm going fifty. One day he would complain that I was going too fast and needed to slow down; the next day, we could be going down the same road, using the same speed, and I wasn't going fast enough. There were several situations where this inconsistency kept me off guard.

Narcissistic Qualities That Invaded Your Marriage and Relationship

Manipulation around the sex in our marriage was very evasive. The fact that he seemed more interested in other women really tore down my self-esteem. The times he left my three-year-old daughter and me while he went to be with his female coworker really hurt me emotionally.

His lack of fiscal responsibility in the ten years of our marriage, we owned at least eleven cars. Each time, we rolled the debt of the previous vehicle into the new car load. It didn't matter if I didn't feel comfortable with a purchase. If he wanted it, he would get it.

His anger and short temper were ever present in our marriage. Everything usually ended in yelling and screaming, doors being slammed, and several times, property damage.

Your Definition of Narcissistic Abuse and/or Abandonment

Narcissistic abuse is the harm that is done in a relationship through various tactics of manipulation and deception where the abuser knowingly controls the victim. It is a process designed to control the victim by decreasing their self-esteem, mental health, and security.

Once the game is done, the abuser will leave the victim with little to no warning.

The End

Mental, Physical, Financial, Emotional Traumas You Experienced

I have been working on building up my self-esteem ever since the marriage ended. I found myself in a second marriage with a man with a very similar personality. After my second divorce, I spent some time working on myself.

Fifteen years since my second divorce, I am excited to seriously be open to a new life partner. In thinking about a new partner, there are times where I really wonder if a man will treat me well. I know I am emotionally in a different place; I won't attract the same type of man as before.

Shame was a big thing for me. I really felt like used goods. I was ashamed of the sexual relations I had. There was also shame around the fact that I fell for this relationship.

Steps You Took toward Recovery, Repair, or Restoration

I have had much counseling as well as building my relationship with God. The counseling has given me very practical understanding of the dynamics at play and my part in the dysfunction.

Working on my relationship with God has helped me to believe and embody that I am special. I am fearfully and wonderfully made; I deserve to be loved and cherished by my husband.

Expectations for the Family after Abandonment/Desertion

Most people don't believe that abandonment and desertion occur, unless they spend some time learning about the dynamics of the narcissistic relationship.

Like any abusive relationship, many people will say, "Why did *you* let it happen? I would have been out of there a long time ago." Or even, "I don't know why *you* didn't see what was going on."

Many times, hearing things like this retraumatizes the victim.

In the relationship, the gaslighting was designed to make the victim question their own reality. Innocently, family and friends can retrigger those feelings of not being heard or believed.

Protecting Oneself from Such an Occurrence

Get to a place of loving yourself and not being a people pleaser.

Learn what you like and dislike.

Try new things.

Strengthen your relationship with God and with other girlfriends.

Be firm in knowing your boundaries. If they are not respected, leave. If you are lonely, build other relationships.

Don't be desperate in the dating game. Even if your biological clock is ticking or you are tired of being single or everyone else is getting married, don't just accept poor or inappropriate behavior so you don't have to be alone. When the relationship starts going downhill, you will wish you were alone!

Listen to those close friends around you. Really listen to when you hear the same thing from more than one person.

Trust your gut. If you can sense things aren't right, get out!

Bible Scriptures Instrumental in Helping You Move Forward

> "Do not be afraid; you will not be put to shame. Do not fear disgrace: you will not be humiliated. You will forget the shame of your youth and remember no more the reproach of your widowhood. For your Maker is your husband—the Lord Almighty is his name—the Holy One of Israel is your Redeemer; he is called the God of all the earth. The Lord will call you back as if you were a wife deserted and distressed in spirit—a wife who married young, only to be rejected," says your God. (Isaiah 54:4–6)

> I praise you because I am fearfully and wonderfully made: your works are wonderful; I know that full well. (Psalm 139:14)

Encouragement for Someone Facing This Devastation Now

Seek counseling with someone who specializes in working with the victims of narcissism.

Be kind to yourself. You have been through a lot. It isn't going to get better overnight, but it will get better.

Do not respond to him right away. This is mainly if there are children involved and you are required to interact with him. If he texts or calls, set a limit that you can't respond for a minimum of two hours.

Did You Seek Counseling for Yourself and Your Daughter?

Yes. I have been in counseling on and off over the past sixteen years. My daughter has received counseling as well.

*****

Red Flags

With my second marriage, I always say, "There wasn't a single red flag...*they were all large red banners being pulled by helicopters and airplanes!*"

1. Yes! Neither husband love-bombed my parents; my parents saw through both of my exes charades. My second husband love-bombed my daughter by giving her a room in his house, playing and joking with her; all this stopped the day we got married.
2. With both, there was a push to get married. My first husband planned a phenomenal proposal—one that was kind of too good to have any other reaction than *yes*. It was on the first year anniversary of our first date. We were living together and kind of talking about marriage, but I wasn't expecting it at all. After the proposal, things were very tense with the wedding planning. He was really pushing to make sure the wedding happened.
3. With my second husband, we had only been dating for about four months. I was afraid he was going to propose to me on Valentine's Day. I confronted him first and told him I wasn't ready for marriage. He got very mad at me for even saying that. We got married three months later.
4. Giving more information than I was given was more an issue with my second husband than my first, and it might

have been because I wasn't really asking questions. I was so desperate for love I was willing to take whatever came my way.

5. My first husband and I went to premarriage counseling. When he didn't do the homework or when he was called on the carpet for his behaviors, his *go-to* excuse was, "But you know I love you, right? So why do you need me to do that to show you?"

6. My first husband was not one to always say the right things or try too hard. My second husband, however, threw my daughter an amazing fifth birthday party. The party had all the works—all her friends, a piñata, all the decorations. We got married shortly after that party. He was very emotionally abusive toward my daughter after that.

7. I was wife number 5 or 6 for my second husband; that depends, though, on whether or not you counted the annulment he had. When we started dating, neither of our divorces was final. Once, I even ran into his soon-to-be ex-wife because she hadn't yet moved out of the house. With each of his marriages, he placed all fault on his ex-wives.

8. My first ex-husband had a very toxic and cyclical relationship with his mother. I had a good relationship with her. When they were fighting, he would try to pit the two of us against each other.

9. I only met my second ex-husband's family at the wedding. We dated for six months and were married for ten months.

10. Both ex-husbands seemed eager to make the marriage official.

11. My first ex-husband violated many boundaries in regard to my time with my family, friends, when I needed to stay late for work, etc. When we met, I was fresh out of college. So when I moved into my first apartment, he just basically moved in with me…even though that wasn't the plan.

12. My second ex-husband was overbearing when it came to my relationship with my daughter. Four at the time, he would get upset with how needy she was for me. He also

didn't like the fact that her father was still in the picture. He actually asked me to sign away my parental rights to my daughter so he didn't have to deal with my ex anymore. That was one of the things that made me leave the second marriage.

13. Additional red flags:
- Rude to waitstaff.
- Short-tempered.
- Aggressive driving.
- Making his situation so much worse than mine. When I would ask him to do something, many times his reaction was, "I can't because I am so busy." This was usually said while he was sitting on the couch.
- Not allowing me to have an opinion or making my choice wrong or bad. When we first started dating, my parents were going to purchase a car for me as a gift for graduating from college. Instead of getting the car I wanted, he pushed me to get the care he wanted...even down to the color.

Kaleema—The Wedding Anniversary Vacation

Interview conducted by Beatrice Bruno (editor, author, consultant)

Demographics

Age: 53
Race/Ethnicity: African American
Occupation: Policy analyst
Religion: Islam
Wife number 4

Red Flags

Red flag no. 1—Ready for marriage or commitment immediately, over-the-top love confessions and accolades, image-/ego-boosting, love-bombing

Red flag no. 2—Asking for more information than he was giving; unexplained gaps in relationships, family, or community; gaps in ties to religious organization

Red flag no. 4—Always says the right thing or tries a bit too hard; mimics thoughts, hopes, and dreams; creates bonds too soon; confesses love to everyone; well rehearsed

Red flag no. 5—Blames ex-wives for demise of marriages, some family members coddle and cover for him, no accountability for his actions

Red flag no. 6—Negative comments about family, manipulates interactions with family

Red flag no. 8—Violates boundaries

The Wedding Anniversary

In this study, we will again address the three segments of the abusive cycle: beginning, middle, and end and how this relates to the process of love-bombing, demeaning/spirit-breaking, and abandonment.

The Beginning

Kaleema shared that her son had an assignment in summer camp to write about the person he admired the most. He wrote about his stepfather, the man who would later abandon him. Her son was in the hotel when they were abandoned by the man who professed to love her son like his own blood. This pain he caused her son, she says, was the ultimate betrayal and trauma, because as an adult, her self-image is already formed, but for a developing child, his image of himself is yet to be seen. She shares that her final words to him was to ask if he was going to at least say goodbye to her son. He kept walking.

Response from His Family

There were mixed emotions within his family on how he had treated my son and me. Two of his family members were shocked and hurt, and others did not care. Maybe because—as I would come to learn—he had done something like this at least once before. I guess his family might have thought that this was par for the course for him. They were only two that seemed to be in shock and showed empathy and asked what they could do for my son and me. Their hurt was also clear and evident.

The response seemed to be more disappointment than shock. He had told me himself that one of them said to him, "Be sure you are ready to get married because she is a single mom, and you don't want to do anything to disrupt her son's life." At the time, I thought it was just concern for my son and blending families. I didn't know it was an omen to what was to come.

The responses his family member gave to me when I called, abandoned on the vacation, made it clear that she was already aware of his plans because she was not surprised. The family member callously and uncaringly said, "Well, he must have been frustrated." I thought to myself, *That is not the response of a person who is hearing this for the first time (now or in the past).* I was calling to say he had left us on our anniversary vacation and we didn't know his whereabouts, and the family member said, "Well, he must have been frustrated..." The family member did not ask any questions like "What happened?" I began to realize that had I said he blackened my eye, the family member would have said, "Then stop running into his fist." It was useless.

After this incident, his family members who were supposedly closest to me, the one who ended every encounter and/or phone call with "I love you," did not call to check on my son and me except once to berate me. The family member called to say that "he left because you were paying more attention to the kids than to him on the vacation and he just doesn't want you anymore, nah, nah, nah." Nah, nah, nah? Really? I thought I was in the twilight zone! What happened to wisdom? Even this call didn't come until months later when I filed a formal complaint against him to the Muslim community.

Did You Have Any Type of Warning—Red Flags in the Beginning?

When I told a close friend about the abandonment, she said, "Why didn't you tell me that something was wrong?" How could I? For three years, eleven months, and three weeks, I was married to *one* person. Then for three days, there was a person that I didn't recognize; day 4, our anniversary, he gave me a card where he handwrote, "Thank you for four wonderful years of marriage." And two days later, they (the stranger and my husband) were gone. I learned that he had done this Dr. Jekyll and Mr. Hyde before…

In hindsight, there were plenty of warnings *before and during* our marriage. First, I was not looking for a husband. I had been divorced for eight years and was not actively looking for a husband as I was finally back on my feet. He, on the other hand, was very adamant and aggressive about marrying me. He mirrored all my likes, dislikes, hopes, dreams, aspirations, fears, wants, and needs. He told me that he wanted me to be his wife during our *first* conversation. He was constantly over the top in front of others, expressing his love. Second, I never met any of his friends or colleagues to establish relationships, only in passing. I had friends and colleagues who would visit the home, and I encouraged his communication with them. Next, after we decided to get married, he retired from his job abruptly, although I told him several times we could commute until one of us could move. We were only living three hours apart. I told him specifically not to leave his job, but he retired abruptly, took a job several levels below him, came to where I was living, and said, "Anything for the family." Four years later, the week prior to the abandonment, he threw this in my face and said, "I made a sacrifice for you." At that time, I knew nothing about narcissism, manipulation, predatory behavior, and abandonment, so I was clueless to what this type of behavior, all these red flags, meant.

I was set up for failure many times. For instance, he told me that he had to drop his family member off at another family member's work for an event, saying several times that his family member was making a big deal of it but that it was nothing important. It happened to be on the same day of a family outing we planned at the beach. He said he would be right back, but when I saw he put on a suit, I said, "You're pretty dressed up just to drop her off." He said (with irritation at her request), "She wants me to walk her inside. She is always making a big deal about nothing. I will be right back." He was gone for several hours. When he returned, we went to a wonderful family day at the beach with my son. A week or so later, I called his family member while I was waiting to see my dad at the nursing home. She asked me why I had not attended a very important event for the family member who received a big award! I was taken by surprise and embarrassed. I told her I did not know about the award. I was quite embarrassed that it seemed to her that I had blown off a very important day for his family member. I was also shocked to find out that she did not know about his event in two days as I have been planning it for two months. I repeatedly told him to be sure to invite his family. Each time, he said that he had forgotten but would get around to it. Another incident was, when I retired, I kept asking him when he was going to tell his family member because it was definitely a cause for celebration. He kept telling me he did not want to tell her because he did not want her to worry about our financial situation. I said it was a retirement; it was not like I got fired. He insisted that she would worry and I should not tell her because I was busy caring for my father, who was often bedridden. I eventually moved on from this after several attempts.

Another "setup" was when we had a Kwanza gathering at our home. We decided we would not exchange gifts with each other but would instead jointly give gifts for our guests. He presented me with *lots* of various gifts. I was embarrassed that I had nothing for him. When I said that we had decided to not exchange gifts between us, his family member said with irritation in her voice, "I would just be appreciative of the gifts." And I was further embarrassed. These seemed like small things, but learning about the art of narcissism and manipulation, I now see that these are the small setups that alienate you from family and friends and give them a false impression of you and/or the marriage. In hindsight, I was set up like this too many times to count.

The days and weeks leading up to his abandonment provided no warning signs because we were carrying on in our normal routines. In hindsight, I recall that he started having "phone problems" two weeks prior. He claimed that Verizon said it would take two weeks to get the new sim card. When I said that didn't sound right, I could tell from his look that this was going to lead to yet another outburst as this had been the routine all week. Well, of course, the two weeks never came because he was gone by the end of that week. It was not until the week of the abandonment that he was like Dr. Jekyll and Mr. Hyde, each day bringing a new persona and a new disruption on his part. He was also looking around the house for things that had not yet been unpacked from the move because they would not be needed immediately. I would just say to check the garage, the upstairs storage closet and go on about my business of caring for my father. He was going through my closet, which was unusual. I asked, "What are you looking for?" He said his graduation robe, which would never be in *my* closet, and he asked about the passports. We had not traveled at all since before COVID and definitely not out of the country. In hindsight, I know now that he was gathering these items two to three weeks prior, preparing for the abandonment. I now know that this is the game of the narcissist, secrecy, creating arguments as a distraction, and gaslighting. But I was a wife who trusted her husband, so I never questioned him as long as it seemed he was taking care of responsibilities. I was caring for my father in the home, and he was often bedridden, so between that, my son, my own job (which was high stress), and my business that I share with my sister, I didn't have time to investigate the activities of a grown man who was supposed to be trustworthy. Although I had caregivers for my father coming and going periodically, this was a blessing and a curse because it was during COVID shutdown, so my priority was keeping the family safe and making sure everyone was healthy all while taking care of my responsibilities.

What Happened Leading Up to the Abandonment?

Five days prior to the abandonment, he began creating multiple reasons to argue with me or "poke" me that didn't make sense. For instance, that Sunday, I called to say I was unexpectedly with my sister and brother-in-law in the hospital. He insisted I stay and take care of the family and said to send them his prayers. When I arrived home, he was distant and visibly angry. When I asked about his mood, he yelled that I was gone all day and began to verbally attack me. He continued, now standing over me while I was sitting, still yelling at me, saying, "You are always whining, always complaining." And he began to mock me with a whinny voice imitating a "white woman." I had never seen him behave this way, and we had *never* had an argument other than slight disagreements. I was confused, wondering what was wrong with him. When I looked confused about his exaggerated behavior, he said, "Since you have that stupid look on your face…!" I finally verbally defended myself, which, in hindsight, allowed him to intensify the argument.

I left the living room because he kept escalating the argument, and my son's room was next to the living room. He followed me to the bedroom, but once we were inside when I tried to close the door, he put his foot in the door. I thought he was confused, so I told him that I was trying to close *us* into the room so my son couldn't hear this ridiculous argument, but he continued to kick/block the bottom of the door with his foot. I finally told him to stop because he could hit me with the door. I was shocked, confused, a bit frightened because we had never argued before, and I couldn't figure out what was happening. In hindsight, I realized he was trying to make me react physically, but I didnt. I say that because later this was the story that he tried to tell my uncle, that he thought he was going to have to put his hands on me because I was confrontational. After this incident that he orchestrated, he gave me the silent treatment for two days, then gifts for the wedding anniversary that included a card in which he wrote, "Alhamdulillah [all praise to God], thank you for four wonderful years of marriage." And then we went to Myrtle

Beach, where he abandoned us. The entire week of the anniversary, including the gifts, was a setup.

We left for our anniversary trip, then on the way, I was speaking with my brother-in-law on speakerphone about our attempt to buy a building for a masjid. We were not in agreement about the strategy. My husband was not in the conversation, but toward the end, he chimed in, in agreement with me. But as soon as I hung up the phone, I asked him, "Is it me, or am I confused?" He started yelling at me at the top of this lungs while I was driving and my son was on the back. "Yes, it's you! It's always you!" Again, this behavior was out character but extremely angry and frightening to experience this while driving down the interstate. He was really yelling. I looked back at my son while I was driving, and I was relieved that he had on headphones, but I was sure he could still hear. We finally arrived at Myrtle Beach without additional incident. By this time, my mind was fried. That night, he was not talking to anyone and strangely sat at the table with his back to me while he, my son, and nephew ate dinner.

In hindsight, it seems that prior to our wedding anniversary/family vacation, he had already determined in his heart that he was going to abandon my son and me. I later learned from his written discovery statement that he had reserved a rental car on that Friday; however, we didn't arrive at our vacation location until Friday night. Then he woke up usually early for a vacation, saying he had to get a toothbrush for my nephew, who was with us in the hotel. He was gone for a very long time, stating that they didn't have any in the hotel and he had to find a Walmart. Since he was unusually quiet and distant while we were all on the beach that night, coupled with his previous "blowups," I said to him that it seemed to be a lot of stress, but this was our anniversary and our first vacation since COVID and we should make the best of it. I then suggested that when we return home, we should seek counseling so we could get help deal with the stress. I think of COVID and caring for my dad in the home and just really still being newlyweds.

He suddenly blew up...*again*, saying that he was not going to counseling and that we need to separate. I was shocked, mouth wide open! He said "I am going home on the bus!" and turned and picked up his suitcase (that was surprisingly already packed) and began to walk out. The only thing I said at that point was, "Are you going to a least say goodbye to my son?" But he kept walking!

That was our last conversation...ever. On that day, I had to suppress all my feelings because my son and nephew were with me. This suppression gave me a headache, and my stomach was in knots. They didn't hear the conversation—it was not even an argument— because they were playing video games in the siting area of our hotel suite that was separated by a kitchenette and we were talking in low tones, not the loud physically aggressive argument he later tried to report to family and friends. I gathered them up and told them that it was time to start our day and that we were going to ride go-carts. I told them that he had an emergency at home and needed to leave. They asked lots of questions, and of course, nothing I said made sense because this whole situation did not make sense. I thought that he was going home. I called my sister and she advised me to stay calm and talk to him when I get home the next day. I didn't want to snatch the kids up and add to the drama/trauma.

When it was time to leave the hotel to go ride go-carts, I realized I didn't know where my car was parked. I texted him to ask him where he parked my car, and he did not respond for six hours. My son and nephew were excited with the "game" of finding my car using the online locator. I had no idea that he created this argument with me to leave the hotel, return to our home, and clear the house of his belongings while my son and I slept, unaware of what was going on at home. While driving home from two states away where he abandoned my son and me, I texted him to say that the pet boarding facility called and our pet was still there and asked if he was going to pick her up before closing. I could not figure out why she would be there if he had been home for the last day and a half. He responded, "Are you asking me or telling me?" I did not respond because I did not want to argue, and I was driving seven hours in a storm to get home to find out what was going on with him. I arrived home just three hours later only to find that he had cleared out all his personal belongings from the home, including passport, documents to our second home, even books from the shelves. Yet he responded to my question about the pet with a question, never saying, "I have moved out."

He later said in discovery statements that he did not intend to divorce until I filed the complaint to the community. However, he left us in the hotel two states away, went home, and took all his things while we were sleeping, with no word of where he would be staying. I didn't file my complaint to the community until sixty days later with still no word from him. With the abandonment and no contact, I filed for divorce.

It sounds like a lifetime, but *all* this happened in five days! Our life—my son and me—unraveled in five days! I didn't know why this was happening, and I didn't know how to protect my son. On Wednesday, he said, "I love you. Happy Anniversary!" and *wrote* to me, "Alhamdulillah [all praise to God]! Thank you for four wonderful years of marriage." And then he was gone. Dr. Jekyll and Mr. Hyde. I am fifty-two; he is sixty-two. And this is not the life and behavior of people who have spent more than half a century on this planet. I was confused, and the only explanation I received after the abandonment was a response to my email asking him to explain his actions. He said, "I won't bother to explain it to you because you wouldn't understand." To add insult to injury, he implied that I was stupid…again. But I recalled that he always said he was the smartest person in the room—any room. So there's that. He never contacted us again and immediately blocked me on social media. The next time I saw him was when I took him to court.

First Feelings/Emotions Experienced after Realization of Abandonment

When my son and I arrived home, the house had been cleared of his belongings. It was as though he had never been there, we were never married, and we were never a family. It was almost as if he had died while we were on our vacation. I imagine that when people go on vacations and someone is fatally injured, robbed, and killed or kidnapped, this is what they come home to. The person that I knew, the person that was being a loving husband just five days before was no more, perhaps never really existed.

At first, I remained silent. I did not know what to say to my son who loved this man dearly. I walked outside because the air inside the house was tight. I was pacing back and forth, trying to think. How was I going to have to tell my son that the man he loved was gone without warning, and how had I entrusted my son to this person that could be so cruel and inhumane not to me but to my *son*? I vomited in the yard. I was unable to sleep for several months. Every time I attempted to close my eyes, I saw and heard my son yelling in his anguish. Every time I attempted to eat, I would feel sick again.

I had been left with the feeling that I woke up one morning and found a stranger had crawled through my window and gotten into my bed and put a gun to my head. I felt unsafe all the time. Who was I sleeping next to each night? I was left with the feeling of being uneasy everywhere I went. This abandonment caused me to rethink my life and I had caused this devastation for my son. I gave unconditional love and trust, and I had caused this devastation not just for me but also for my son. It was horrific! I had all these thoughts that night and woke up the next morning to start my new job at 8:00 a.m. He also knew this; it was part of the reason we took the vacation, because with my new job, I would not be able to take leave for a while. It was our anniversary. I had recently retired from twenty-two years in federal government, and I was exhausted from caring for my father. These were all the reasons he took us to Myrtle Beach that faithful weekend. I started work, again suppressing my feelings, and showed up on the job the next day as if nothing had happened. I was stuffing my feelings deep down and it was eating me. I worked daily on the job, caring for my dad and my other responsibilities like a robot. Several people asked me if this might have been a result of the mounting responsibilities of caring for my father, but the idea to move to accommodate my father was not my idea. I was very happy to do it, but I didn't want to suggest it because I didn't want my husband to feel pressured to agree. However, when he suggested the idea, I jumped right on it 100 percent. In hindsight, perhaps it was just to get back to his own stomping grounds.

Your Son's Experience

When I shared with my son that the man he had come to love so much had left us, he was devastated in a way I had not seen since the death of my mother. He had adored this man. If he put on camouflage pants, my son would go find his camouflage pants and so on. He would try to imitate him in many ways. He often said that he was more than a stepfather to him. Now the same man who had treated him like his own son was gone in a flash without a goodbye. My son did not know how to process this new information. Everything was *not okay*. In my son's young mind, his stepfather had just left but would come back. After he calmed down with me, he went room to room to see where his stepfather's things had been as if he could not believe what I was telling him. There was *nothing there*! The sound of his agony would be a sound that would jar me awake for several months afterward.

This man orchestrated this cruelty without any thought of my son. There was nothing happening to prevent him from doing this civilly and talking to my son to say he was leaving. There was nothing to prevent him from saying we shouldn't take this trip at all. With my son and my nephew in the hotel with us, he knew I would not protest his actions because I wouldn't want to upset the boys. Therefore, this whole conversation was had in hushed tones. His timing was well planned out.

After it was over, I told my son that we, as Muslims, cannot compel someone to stay or go. But as Muslims, there is a way we must go about doing things. I told my son if he wanted to leave, he has every right, but he doesn't have the right to do it the way he did without care and with malice. It was not a crime of passion; it had been planned out. This was not something I could have prepared my son for because he continued the narrative of us finally taking a long-awaited family vacation. His actions were intentional and inflicted great emotional and psychological harm on my son. My son was traumatized by the shock of his departure—this man whom my son wrote about saying he admired more than anyone in the world. My son was collateral damage of this man's selfishness and lack of care for a minor child. This was an act that had the capability of devastating my son in ways I could have never imagined.

When it was all said and done, my son said, "He treats marriage like a game." That from a thirteen-year-old! I won't go into too much detail about my son's experience because it is his story to tell when and if he should decide to tell it. But I will say this, I am proud of my son, and he is a true soldier. My son will be a better person because we have talked extensively about empathy, compassion, and responsibility. Our biggest life lessons come from adversity. I pray to the Creator that my son will grow to be a man who has integrity and strength and, most of all, faith and trust in Allah.

First Response of Your Family and Those in Religious or Social Circles

My family was in disbelief, shocked, and angry. They had also trusted him and entrusted their children to him as well. Some treated me as if I had been widowed. People were coming and going from my home, sitting in solace, bringing food, offering comfort. Some of family members are still dealing with anger over what he did. Some of my family members were asking themselves what they missed, what they could have done, why he didn't come to them if he was having a problem. Others were all reciting the things that just didn't feel right about him and recounting all the times they wanted to express it but wanted to hope for the better. But I learned from my research that that is the art of the narcissists, getting everyone to blame themselves for his actions.

Some of those inside and outside of my Muslim community faced and experienced the same emotional upheaval my son and I faced. People called me to express their shock. They were now afraid to trust their own judgment because my spouse was considered a reputable person in the community. But as dots started to get connected, it was the same as my family…that they knew something wasn't quite right.

When he deserted us, family and congregation members asked what my son and I needed. I replied that I didn't need anything; I was just in a fog, and when the fog lifted, there was nothing to see but a string of lies that just did not connect. Family and community members silently and anonymously slipped money to me and sent gift cards. I said "No, thank you" more times than I could count until a brother told me that he just had to do something…as a man, that he could just not stand by and do nothing. It was then that I understood that they had also been deceived and had to find a way to ease their own pain as well. I delayed telling some family because I didn't want them to be hurt by what he did. In the end, they were hurt anyway because they loved and accepted him too.

Symptoms of Grief and When It Set In

The grief was immediate and prevailing. The anxiety was ongoing, invasive, and constant. To compound things, I was still caring for my eighty-three-year-old father in the home, and now he needed hospice care, so I returned to the empty house, a new job the next day, and organizing hospice care for my dad. Six weeks later, my dad passed away, and I was numb having to take on both things at once and work full-time and caring for my son. I never received condolences on the death of my father from my husband or his family. I had already learned after the fact from his ex not to expect to hear anything. I was doing all this without sleeping, eating, or resting. In essence, someone had died; *two* someones in my life had died. Extreme grief set in when recalling my son's yelling out as a response to the realization that all of his stepfather's things were gone and kept me awake night after night. I knew I was suffering but did not immediately realize it was a form of PTSD. I had multiple traumas back-to-back with no relief in sight. I did reach out to counseling from a private Muslim-based counseling service (a husband-and-wife team), and I had received work-related counseling. It was a lifeline for me. I tried hard to maintain a stable environment for my son. My male family members jumped in to fill in the gaps for my son, because as hard as I tried to be, I was not 100 percent, not even 50 percent, of who I was before the trauma. On top of all of that, when he abandoned us, he said that he would pay the mortgage—as was our routine financial setup—but then said he would only pay one month even though Islamicly and legally, he was responsible for quite a bit more. My poor father offered to pay, but I refused. I was supposed to be taking care of *him* during his old age and sickness, not the other way around. It wasn't until I took him to court that I was able to get spousal support. Even then, he tried to get out of it, saying I had a larger income. But we had numerous financial obligations to two homes (one of which he tried to sell, claiming it was his alone), and I was caring for my father as well. We planned together for me to retire, discussing all our finances and then he left the day before my new job! It was clear that he intended to leave me holding the bag…to drown.

One must still adhere to your Islamic obligations or make a plan for separation, not just run out. Sisters, make sure you get an attorney. *Do not* try to be your own attorney! I was able to file for divorce on the grounds of abandonment and desertion and request my maintenance/support. Sisters, please check the laws in your state even at the point of the marriage contract or prenuptial agreement to make sure you are specific and get all your rights! My attorney told me if I had a signed agreement on the front end, we would not have had that struggle. But it is also likely that had I pressed this and other issues that we would not have been married in the first place.

The Middle

Advice to Other Women about Your Experience

- Do your homework no matter his confessions of love, his religion, or his perceived social standing.
- Ask more questions.
- A background check will be invaluable.
- Be aware of the absence of close friends or colleagues and distancing from his family.
- Do not be the rebound person.
- Check out the man behind the mask.

- Beware of the person that appears to be the perfect soul mate, that everything you want or need is what they want or need.
- Beware of quick courtships.
- Go to his home and find out what is going on there. You should do this very early on because his "revolving" door of relationships can be exposed. If he doesn't allow this, it's very likely he is still with a current wife or relationship.

Some Telltale Signs That a Person Is Being Groomed for Abandonment

The narcissist will groom you. The abuse will be subtle and will seem like mistakes or slips of the tongue and will be explained away as a bad day, or apologies and gifts will be used for a cover-up. The abuse will come more frequently or pronounced as time goes on. He will test you with small things to see if you will go along. My spouse one night ordered nonalcoholic beer. It became a source of contention as I complained that it still had alcohol. Also, we are Muslim, and it gives a distorted image of passersby about our lifestyle. He had the waitress put in another glass (and I continued to complain). But he kept it, and I, not wanting to ruin our date night, let it go. He never did it again, but this was (I came to learn) one of the many tests I was to "pass or fail" in the art of manipulation *or* just a glimpse behind the mask.

Questions You Regret Not Asking

- ✓ My biggest mistake was not a question that I did *not* ask but the fact that I did not follow up on his answer. I asked him what his family thought about us getting married because it was pretty quick, and he said, "They are happy, but my family member [he called the name] told me to be 100 percent sure that I am ready to get married because you are a single mother and seem to be doing well, and she wouldn't want me to do anything to disrupt your son's life." Tragically, I assumed the comment was in relation to blending families and the struggles that can come with that. I thought this was very sweet of her (and she is a sweet person still); however, my mistake was not following up on what she actually meant. Now in hindsight, after the abandonment and then finding out that he had abruptly left the previous marriage, I believe that her statement had a lot more to do with his actions in his previous marriage just before me. Ironically, that family member was the first person whom I called upon arriving home and finding out that he had moved all his things out. When I was describing to her what happened over the course of the vacation and what I was looking at now—a house that showed no sign of him ever being there—I said it was almost (and we said simultaneously), "Like it was orchestrated."

✓ I did ask multiple times how he felt about "starting over" with a teenager since all his children were out of school. This was probably the thing I asked most often, but with him countering with his work with boys with absentee fathers, he gained my confidence that this marriage would be good for my son. He insisted countless times that he was excited about having a teenager in the house and definitely excited about having a son to do things with. In the end, he walked off even when I asked if he was going to say goodbye to my son. I was shocked because even if he grew to hate me for some reason, what about my son? He just kept walking. I regret not asking more about his treatment of children in the past.

✓ How did your last three marriages end (and get verification)? Ask this question especially if he blames everything on the ex-wives and *verify*! Don't just take his word for it.

✓ Can I speak with your ex-wife? This one conversation could have saved me and my son so much heartache. I spoke with her for the first time after the abandonment only to learn she had found my engagement ring in the process of him discarding their marriage. It was shocking to hear her story almost identical to mine. His "process" was the same, but the things he indulged in, such as alcohol, was totally opposite from our way of life. It was unbelievable how, on multiple occasions, during this conversation that she was completing my sentences and I was completing hers. But the person she described was someone very foreign to our way of life.

✓ Why are you leaving your current job so abruptly and relocating to live in the state in which I reside? I received a response that didn't sit well because it was not what a reasonable person would do, especially since I was saying that I was okay with a "commuter marriage" to save him from leaving his job. We were both nearing eligibility for retirement, so we need to play smart and safe, not to be rash in our decisions at this point in life, me nearing fifty and him nearing sixty.

✓ How long have you been in your current Muslim community?

✓ Where were you in times of absence from the Muslim community? Can anyone vouch for your whereabouts/lifestyle?

✓ I regret not asking to spend time with and/or meet his close friends. In hindsight, I realize that he had no close friends, colleagues, or fraternity brothers at our wedding. My friends and colleagues came to our home from time to time. It's true that some people are loners, but I really regret not insisting I meet his friends and fraternity brothers whom he seemed to meet with regularly when we were in courtship.

Narcissistic Qualities That Invaded Your Marriage and Relationship

The narcissist never changes his patterns.

1. *Love-bombing.* He will act like you are the best thing since heaven opened up! He will do and be everything that you need and swear that he eats, sleeps, and drinks every bit of you. Now that your guard is down, he will love, hate, and

want everything you love, hate, and want. He will mirror your emotions like a puppet on a string. You will think to yourself, *This is the male version of me. He is my soul mate!* He actually said to me one day, "Although I'm from Philly, you don't have to worry about me. I'm not like those brothers in Philly!" (implying about how they are known for abandonment).

2. *Diminishing.* He will slowly start to show signs of diminishing you. He will make small backhanded comments that will be brushed off as a bad day to diminish an accomplishment. When I turned down a job that was going to be a huge pay cut, he angrily said, "How much money do you need anyway? I would have to work two jobs to get that money!" He was trying to make me feel ashamed for demanding my worth. Where he once always offered advice, now he will snap at you when you come to him, because now you are too needy. He will try and turn you against your family or friends and make small comments about them that say they are not good enough or make you think they are against you in some way. He will attempt to make you second-guess yourself. Then there will be the silent treatment. This is a double-edged sword: to punish you for something that you are not aware of, reel you in, then snap at you and say you are hovering if you ask about his well-being.

3. *Disappearing act.* This may be gradual for hours, or maybe it will come all at once, like in my case. In hindsight, in the last few weeks, he would be gone for several hours regularly, saying he was working late or visiting his family, but since I was caring for my dad, I didn't question it (or even have time), and also, I was putting blind trust that his word was good enough.

Your Definition of Narcissistic Abuse and/or Abandonment

- According to the law, abandonment is leaving the marriage and/or marital home without warning or justification. Abandonment means to walk away from your spouse, family, home without a warning, no conversation to say, "This is going to happen. We are going to separate." Desertion is doing the same while also withdrawing financial support.
- Manipulation, lies, cheating.
- The perpetrator is usually addicted to something: drugs, alcohol, sex, porn, OCD behavior. I was told that he showed obsessive behavior to multiple things that were outside of our way of life regularly in his previous marriage, where he freely engaged in these things.
- Mood swings. There were times during which my son and I would walk on eggshells. Then all would be right with the world, and the cycle would continue. I would explain this away to my son, saying that some people are not used to having a busy home with family and friends coming and going and to just give space. However, after the abandonment, I learned that in his previous marriage, like clockwork, on a routine basis, the mood swings would set in, and he would blow up, be distant, return, and start again. I really regret not being more inquisitive and asking follow-up questions and getting firsthand information. I could have saved myself (and especially my son) a lot of trauma and grief.

The End

Emotional, Mental, Physical, and Financial Tolls of Abandonment and Desertion of You, Your children, Your Family

The extent of the emotional, mental, and physical the toll was still unfolding in our lives because our story in many ways is just beginning. There were still lingering questions in my heart and mind causing me to doubt myself, but I know now that is called trauma bonding. I am not sure how I will trust anyone with my son again. The trauma that is inflicted by my ex was unimaginable. Through this situation, I have been forced to become someone I never dreamed of becoming: a little bit more closed off than is my usual nature and second-guessing everyone.

Financially, I had to fight in court for spousal support that is mine to have by the right of the law as well as the laws of Islam. Even then, after I was awarded spousal support, he filed an appeal to deny my maintenance and had yet to say to me what I had done. But what I have learned from my research is, if nothing else, the narcissists don't have to give any reason for their egregious abuse except because "they can." And his exact words, "I won't bother to tell you because you won't understand." Although I presented and listed witnesses for court, he listed not one to attest to whatever reasons he claimed to have for the abandonment. Although he claimed later that he left because I was physically confrontational, he never presented this information in court, which would have probably saved him from paying spousal support, because his only defense to not paying was that my income was higher.

As a Muslim woman, I am entitled to spousal support. I was offered a large sum *but* it came with a condition of not speaking publicly *and* changing the cause of divorce from abandonment and desertion to a no-fault divorce. I was not going to rewrite the truth of what occurred. I did not want anything more than what was owed to me. I would not, *could* not accept money in exchange for dismissing all the emotional trauma that my son and I had endured. He rented a car the day before he disserted us on the vacation; there was no cause for such deception. In the end, I did receive the marital home, 50 percent of the proceeds from the second home, spousal support, and attorney's fees, but this is a case of "when you win, you still lose" because the psychological abuse that my son and I suffered could never be compensated by material things.

Later, I was shocked to see him on social media as guest speaker for a Sunday morning church service, saying that salat (the form of prayer prescribed for Muslims) did not work for him and that any organized religion does not work and "God did not speak to him" until he put down organized religion and embraced spirituality! Be Muslim, be Christian, but most important, be honest and transparent. If you denounce salat, does that make you an apostate?

Steps You Took toward Recovery, Repair, or Restoration

The first step I took was standing up for myself and exposing the abuse. I wrote and filed a formal complaint to the community, and I read my complaint before the congregation. I responded to every question about the incident. This was very hard to do, and I wouldn't wish it on anyone. However, I knew that if I hid what was done to my son and me, I would have to keep hiding and face ridicule due to people coming up with their own explanation of what happened. So I let them get it straight from me and ask whatever they wanted to ask and be done with it.

This is the same process as grief from the death of a loved one or a significant other. The stages of grief all come into play: denial, anger, bargaining, depression, acceptance. You will have PTSD and experience painful thoughts of your ex, especially if it was abrupt, without warning signs. I was immediately in counseling. I learned about PTSD and other emotional traumas that I had suffered and how to work through them. My son also had counseling, and he had lots of support from family and friends. I learned that I cannot be his only support system and that a variety of sources of support is more effective. I learned to lean on "the village." There is always something good to come of something bad. Allah has promised after every hardship, He will give us ease!

Anxiety around the holidays and other events—there was shame in showing up at holidays (Eid, Thanksgiving, New Year's) alone, but I had to remind myself the shame was *his*, if he had any conscience, which, by the looks of it, was a resounding no!

On my father's funeral, people were questioning why he wasn't on the obituary. He didn't deserve a place on my father's obituary. But you must fight the feeling of shame. Just like a woman who is assaulted, raped, or robbed, it is easy to blame yourself, to hold your head down. Rape is an act of power, mostly not a sexual act, and abandonment is also an act of power. I must remember that I was robbed of safety, honesty, trust in the human spirit, an opportunity to shelter my son, and I was robbed of human decency by being left two states away in our pajamas, dumped out like we were disposable. This was lack of decency to the nth degree! It is easy to blame ourselves for not being aware that our own husband was plotting while we slept (literally). I have to remember to say "Stop it!" to myself when I go down this train of thought. Instead, you must document and expose the abuse. Don't become an angry woman, but do become a protector of yourself.

Be meticulous in your documentation and clear about what he has done. I wrote a complaint to the Muslim community charging him with abandonment just as if he had been charged with theft or some other heinous crime (see appendices). This was not the letter of a woman scorned but a formal complaint of a woman who was a victim of a con artist and was demanding her rights as a Muslim! I detailed the crime and stated what the punishment should be and how this can and should be avoided in the future. I hope other sisters can use this information to protect themselves.

I spoke with a counselor immediately that night just before telling my son what happened because I didn't want to be the cause of inflicting additional trauma. I currently see a counselor as I move forward with my life. I recall saying to the counselor that I guess I should consider myself lucky that I didn't wake up with a pillow over my face! She said, "Well, yeah." I didn't want to mention that, but this behavior is not far from that. The fact that all evidence points to that while he was planning this for weeks while he carried on the dutiful husband routine was indeed diabolical.

Expectations for the Family after Abandonment/Desertion

The victim should reach out to those charged with authority in the community. If they do not assist, then reach out to any community. I found support locally and nationally. Write a formal complaint and address it to the community and read it in person and charge the person with the crime. Share this with family as well. Expect them to require him to come in person and account for his actions. If he does not, expect the community to deny his participation. *Expect better!*

Do not marry without a legal marriage license. Yes, you can get the Islamic marriage certificate, but this is not legal in the state and will not protect your rights. He *will* shirk his duty and violate your rights. These men depend on you not making it legal in your state so they can take advantage of you. It is harder to hold them accountable if you don't have the law of the land on your side. The men that will do this will totally disregard Islam. They will tell you do not let the government run your life, but the Quran does tell us to obey the laws of the land as long as they do not conflict with Quran and Sunnah.

My ex used Islam every time he needed to get something he wanted, but when he wanted to abuse the marriage, he was no longer using Islam. I wished I had asked his ex if he practiced Islam in their home.

Quran Scriptures Instrumental in Helping You Move Forward

Your Lord has not forsaken you, nor is He displeased. Definitely, what is to come is better than what has passed. Soon your Lord will grant you, and you will be pleased. (Surah Ad-Duha 93:3–5)

And those who had taqwa of their Lord will be led to Paradise in groups. Until, when they reach it, its doors will be (already) open, and its guards will say: "Peace be upon you! You have done well! So, enter it forever!" (Surah Az-Zumar 39:73)

Allah does not test a soul with more than it can handle. For it is what it has earned and against it is what it has earned. Our Lord do not hold us accountable when we forget or make mistakes. Our Lord do not place on us such burdens like how you placed those before us. Our Lord do not make us bear that which is beyond our abilities. Overlook us, forgive us, and have mercy on us. You are our Lord, so assist us against the disbelieving people. (Surah Al-Baqarah 2:185)

Then Indeed, with difficulty there is ease. Indeed, with difficulty, there is ease. (Surah Al-Inshiraa 94:5–6)

O Allah, Lord of the Seven heavens, Lord of the Magnificent Throne, be for me a support against [say the person's name] and his helpers from among your creatures, lest any of them abuse me or do me wrong. Mighty is Your patronage and glorious are Your praises. There is none worthy of worship but You. (129)

Encouragement for Someone Facing This Devastation Now

You will be distraught. But during that time, you must *think, work, and act quickly*! Trace your steps; trace *his* steps. All criminals leave a trail. Do a background check. Talk to people and connect the dots. Men like these continue to abuse women because they compartmentalize their lives and keep family and friends from talking to each other. Document and then put all the pieces together and *fight*! Do not walk away without demanding your rights! Allah (God) (the law and the religion) is on your side. Stand up for your rights and expose, expose, *expose* the abuse! They do this because they expect you to be quiet and live in shame. Put the shame on them!

In extreme circumstances, you might need to hire an investigator if you experience all the red flags plus the abandonment. You might find that he might be living an alternate life. He is going to tell people that you are paranoid or that you are crazy, but hiring an investigator will put that whole thing to rest, and you will know for sure what you are dealing with and who he really is and his true life behind the mask.

Make sure your marriage is legally documented! I was really in shock. This was the person who sought me out and pursued me relentlessly, said he would never be married again (I was wife number 4), but he swore to me and anyone in earshot that this was forever and got down on one knee and proposed to me. Four years later, this was the same person who took my son and me on an anniversary vacation two states away and left us there, went to the family home, and cleared it of all his things without warning or cause. This was the same person whom the courts had to compel to stop the attempted sale of a home we owned mutually, compel to respond to discovery questions to my attorney, compel to submit his bank and financial statements, compel to pay spousal support. I had no idea who this person was. I advise women to have a legal marriage or a legal marriage contract. Where would I have been without the court process?

*****

Additional Situational Red Flags

1. There were so many red flags in hindsight. In our first conversation, he said that he had been watching me volunteer in the community and that he knew every time he saw me that I would be a perfect wife for him. I told him that I wasn't really looking for a husband at that time. He said that if I gave him a chance, he would show me that he would be a good husband to me and a good support system to my son.

    He began telling me about his work and his books about boys with absentee fathers. He kept emphasizing that he knew that I was a perfect wife for him. I told him that there were many things that some Muslim men might not like about me because I was career-oriented, I was very opinionated, and also, I was not a housewife, but I could maintain the house. But my career was also important to me. He said that this was "perfect for him" because his previous wives were not ambitious enough and that we could be a power couple. I later learned that all his previous wives were accomplished women."

He told me that he had been thinking about me over the course of the previous year. However, I had just lost my mother, and he was giving me time to grieve. I thought this was a sign that he would be caring and compassionate. Had I connected the dots, I would have realized that when my mother passed, he was still with the previous wife.

2. He told me to drop the child support order for my son and he would take care of him and help me even get him through college. This was the same person who walked out on him. At the time, though, I thought that this was just him wanting to make us feel cared for and secure. I was happily providing the information with the thought that if he knew a lot about me and my likes and dislikes, my wants and needs, we could quickly determine if we were on the same page. I thought that this would also give information that would create a successful courtship and/or marriage by being transparent.

Giving me blow by blow of his escapades before becoming Muslim seemed to be a source of pleasure and entertainment for him. The more shocked I was, the more pleased with himself he seemed to be. I would sometimes say, "You probably should have kept that to yourself." I would think to myself that he must be making this up to seem like a "bad boy," not realizing these things were true.

The morning after our nikah [wedding], he told me about extreme substance abuse that included multiple overdoses. At first, I didn't believe it, then I dismissed it because it was so long ago and wasn't a part of his current lifestyle.

He did not explain any gaps from the community. Everyone made assumptions, and he allowed them to assume that when he was absent from one community, he was in a neighboring community. After the fact, when everything was put together, it was realized by all that he was not really working in either community; he was just showing up periodically.

3. When I talked about having a bookstore, he mimicked this dream as well. He said he would support me in this, and he did for a while. Then all of a sudden, he did not, even yelling at me about working at the store, but this was during the week leading up to the abandonment. He talked about wanting to retire together in the location I loved: Myrtle Beach. Unfortunately, Myrtle Beach became the location of the abandonment. He knew I liked going to Myrtle Beach every year for vacation because I love the beach.

    We met family and friends at the African American Museum of History in Washington, DC, I had organized a trip. One of my friends from Atlanta had expressed a little doubt about how fast things were moving. He openly confessed his love for me to all the people there: my friends, my family, people he had not even met before. He did this often in public.

    He did not take any accountability for anything that occurred in any of his marriages. I recall asking him one time, "Do you think if you had backed out of the situation that your exes would have had a better relationship with your family member(s)?" He did not respond.

4. He always cautioned me to stay clear of certain family members so they would not cause drama in our lives or that they would mistreat me because they had mistreated his previous wives. Even when I said I did not think anyone would mistreat me, that I really loved his family and vice versa, he continued to warn me to stay distant from certain family members.

    I often asked him to invite them to come and visit. It would only happen if I persisted. Once we moved near family, I constantly asked him to have them come and visit, to have dinner or cookouts and things of that nature. He would only invite one family member, the same one family member, each time. He would never extend the invitation to other family members that I knew of.

5. We did not talk about doing an Islamic marriage contract. In hindsight, I really regret this. I would never advise anyone to get married without these details spelled out. If you are not going

to get an Islamic marriage contract, you should definitely have a prenuptial agreement. We did not talk about any of these things.

6. I definitely should have spoken to his previous wives before marrying him. Had I spoken to her, I would have found out that he had abruptly left their marriage, requiring her to move out. In fact, I should have spoken to both of his previous wives that were still living. I would also ask about the lifestyle he was leading.

My advice to other women would be, "Follow your gut!" So many times, my gut told me that something was wrong during the love-bombing stage. Instead of following my gut, though, I would tell myself, "We said this would be the last marriage for both of us. We are going to grow old together," which was what he was saying as well. He constantly said we would not divorce no matter what. Yet he left us, never even giving me a reason to this day. So I talked myself out of my doubts and said to myself, "Just enjoy it and trust him." I gave him unconditional trust. I never questioned what he was doing or where he was going. I didn't question any of these things.

I would also advise women to not allow people to become close to their children. Of course, we all say this. But once you get married, then of course, you want to build that type of relationship. My son was devastated and traumatized by this behavior. Because of that, I would definitely ask many, many, many questions. If someone doesn't like my questions, I will be happy to move on.

USEFUL DOCUMENTS

Sample Letter of Complaint

With the Name of Allah, the Merciful Benefactor, The Merciful Redeemer
(بِسْمِ اللهِ الرَّحْمَنِ الرَّحِيْمِ)

> The Prophet Muhammad (PBUH) said, "The believers who show the most perfect faith are those who have the best morals, and the best of you are those who are the best to their wives."

This is an open letter to the leadership of the Hampton Roads Muslim Community of Virginia which includes: W.D. Muhammad Islamic Center of Chesapeake; Masjid William Salaam; The Islamic Center of Tidewater; Masjid Ash Shura, Ansar Mosque and Temple #57 (Norfolk); Crescent Community Center (Virginia Beach); Al'Qubaan Islamic Center (Newport News), and The Hampton Mosque and Peninsula Islamic Community Center (Hampton)

November 10, 2021

As-Salaam Alaikum Brother Imams,

I humbly come before you, the leaders of the Hampton Roads Muslim Community to accept my written complaint against my husband, ████████████████████ for abandonment and desertion of the family. He abandoned us while on a family vacation and our 3rd year wedding anniversary in Myrtle Beach, South Carolina on October 8, 2021. He then traveled 6 hours back to our home in Virginia Beach, Virginia and cleared it of all his possessions while we slept unaware that he was moving out of the family home. We have not seen him or spoken to him since he left us in South Carolina. He has not come forward to account for his actions. I have reached out to him, our leadership and family members (as is the protocol). **Now, I come to you the authority among us to request that he be sanctioned for the egregious violation of my rights as a Muslim, a wife, and a mother.**

He violated the marriage contract which states: *"This Agreement of marriage in accordance with the word of Allah, the Holy Quran and the Sunnah of the Prophet Muhammad (PBUH)"* agreed to and signed on June 15, 2018, by Imam Hosea Abdul-Salaam and three signing witnesses: Imam Ali Abdul Salaam, Sis. Krystal Salaam and Sis. Ellene Ashanti) at the Eid Celebration in Chesapeake, Virginia (and again legally married Oct. 6, 2018).

My rights as a Muslim, a wife and as a mother {(according to The Quran and Sunnah of the Prophet Muhammad (PBUH)}, have been violated in the following ways:

1. he abandoned and deserted the family in South Carolina **without a stated cause, warning, or justification**. *(According to Islamic scholars, abandonment (of one's wife) should not proceed advising her of any issues or failed duties; by Virginia law abandonment is to leave the home/marriage without warning and desertion is defined as abandonment without financial support).*
2. he secretly went to the family home after he left us in S.C. and removed all his possessions.
3. he created an atmosphere of emotional distress for my 13-year-old son who was with me in S.C. when he abandoned us as well as when we returned to the empty home; and
4. he emailed me the next week to say that he would *"only pay mortgage ending in December and nothing else"* which violates my right to maintenance as a Muslim wife, as we are not yet divorced. *(During the marriage he paid the mortgage, and I paid all the remaining joint living expenses including the HOA fees for both homes and his car insurance).* The unexpected withdrawal creates a financial hardship.

KALEEMA OVERTON AMEEN

With the Name of Allah, the Merciful Benefactor, The Merciful Redeemer
(بِسْمِ اللهِ الرَّحْمَنِ الرَّحِيْمِ)

My request to the leadership of the Hampton Roads Muslim Community is as follows:

1. to sanction him by removing his privileges of being the Katib until he provides suitable justification.
2. to hold him accountable for these egregious actions that are in violation of the laws and ethics of Islam; and
3. to request that he comes forward with a justification to me and my family, who was also harmed by his actions.

The Quran implores men to treat women with kindness and respect, even in times of dissent or disagreement. Neither me (nor my son who was under his care) received this consideration. In fact, the only "explanation" was one week later by email stating "…you wouldn't understand so I won't even bother to explain it to you." Am I not an intelligent, thinking human being and worthy of explanation? Good Islamic behavior cannot be enforced, however gross injustice should NEVER be tolerated. Quran 4:35 "And if you fear a separation between the two of them, appoint an arbitrator from his family and an arbitrator from her family...Verily Allah is Knowing, Knowledgeable." and Quran 2:229 "Divorce on reasonable terms and release with kindness...". Neither of these occurred because he did not tell me prior that he wanted to separate, he just left us in South Carolina without warning or justification.

I am coming forward because it is not my shame, but ██████████████ shame for deserting his family without explanation. Living in the shadows of desertion is oppression but stepping into the light will free others by bringing focus to a problem that is often ignored. Desertion and/or abandonment is an area where the rights of Muslim women (and non-Muslim women married Muslim men) are violated and to add insult to injury, ignored. The Community must openly address this issue so victims are not further harmed by the silence, while the perpetrators go free. These gaps in the structure of the community allow for the exploitation, abuse and neglect of women and children. This practice is a crack in the foundation of the Muslim and African American communities, worse if it is done without consequence. We cannot say we are about building family and community life if we are not willing to protect and defend those who are abused and/or neglected (mentally, spiritually, physically, or financially).

██████████████ discarded us like we did not have our God-given rights as Muslims or human beings and without any thought of our safety. He did not even bother to contact us to see if we got home safely from the 7-hour ride in the storm nor did he to contact my family to say that he left us in S.C. so they could check on our well-being. It quickly became apparent that he had *planned* to leave us in South Carolina so he could move out of the family home in secrecy. This is just a summary of what happened to us. I have been made aware that this is not an isolated incident for him. The recently discovered hidden details of his un-Islamic life are not appropriate to share here (as they have legal impact) but will be shared in the proper legal venue, as necessary. ██████████████ knowingly spun a web of lies, deceit and hypocrisy. Abandonment in our community needs to be brought to light so other (so-called Muslims) do not neglect and/or abuse women and children without consequence. His desertion was *clearly planned and premeditated and inflicted psychological and emotional harm* as his actions left me no way to protect or ease the pain for my son. He willingly sacrificed his reputation as a husband, father, leader and Katib; faculty of ██████████████ ██████████ and ██████████████████████ for reasons still unknown.

Again, I petition you as the leaders of the Muslim communities of Hampton Roads, please put a stop to this assault on the dignity of Muslim families ██████████████ must come forward to justify deserting his family in S.C. on our family trip and wedding anniversary and then going to the family home and secretly clearing it out of ALL his possessions while we sleep unaware and abandoned. My son does not deserve to be abandoned by the man

198

With the Name of Allah, the Merciful Benefactor, The Merciful Redeemer
(بِسْمِ اللهِ الرَّحْمَنِ الرَّحِيْمِ)

that he loved dearly and who filled the role of his parent for the last three years, without an explanation. I don't have words to explain the devastation for my son or how a mother hurts for her child. This man, the ███████████ ████████████████████ abandoned us using a pre-meditated and devious plot. This type of deceit, verbal and psychological abuse, and oppression of women while representing Islam must not be tolerated. Where can women and children be protected if not under the banner of Islam? I request that our leadership hold him accountable for this despicable behavior and even more importantly stand against this practice to protect the women and children (Muslim and non-Muslim) that seek protection and security while living beneath the honorable banner of Islam.

The Honorable Imam W.D. Muhammed said, "What we should be concentrating on is establishing ourselves; the whole (Islamic) life and follow our own purpose. That purpose for us now is to obey the law as Muslims following the Quran and the Prophet Muhammad, (PBUH)."

May we all gain knowledge, wisdom and understanding from this shameful assault on family life, inshallah.

Kaleema O. Ameen

Kaleema Overton Ameen
W.D. Muhammad Islamic Center of Chesapeake
KaleemaAmeen@gmail.com

(Resident Imam: Ali Abdul Salaam 757-646-9799)

Sample Prenuptial Agreement

AGREEMENT:

AGREEMENT made this 11th day of September 2014, between W ("W"), (Social Security No.), residing at _____ and A ("A"), (Social Security No.), residing at _____ (sometimes W and A are referred to as the "Parties").

WITNESSETH:

WHEREAS a marriage is contemplated by W and A and

WHEREAS the Parties wish to define and determine their respective rights and obligations with respect to his or her own property and in the property of the other in the event of a dissolution of their marriage regardless of whether their property rights are to be governed by the laws of the State of New York or any other domestic or foreign jurisdiction and

WHEREAS the Parties, to the extent as set forth herein, wish to relinquish any and all rights that either of them may have in the other's separate property as specifically set forth and defined herein, whether acquired prior or subsequent to the marriage and

WHEREAS the Parties hereto have had the opportunity to fully, separately, and independently be apprised and advised of their respective legal rights, remedies, privileges, and obligations that, but for this Agreement, will arise out of the marital relationship or otherwise, by counsel of their own choice and selection and

WHEREAS the Parties each warrant and represent to the other that they and each of them fully understand all the terms, covenants, conditions, provisions. and obligations incumbent upon each of them by virtue of this Agreement to be performed or contemplated by each of them hereunder, and each believes the same to be fair, just, reasonable, and to his or her respective best interests.

Now, THEREFORE, in consideration of the premises and of the covenants, promises, and waivers contained herein, the Parties mutually agree as follows:

ARTICLE I—CONTINGENT AGREEMENT

This Agreement is contingent upon the Parties' contemplated marriage. In the event the marriage does not occur, then this Agreement shall be null and void and of no force or effect.

ARTICLE II—PREAMBLE

The Parties agree that the Preamble is incorporated herein by reference with the same force and effect as if fully set forth herein at length.

ARTICLE III—SEPARATE PROPERTY

A. The following shall constitute the Parties' Separate Property:

1. The property listed on Schedule A as A's property and on Schedule B as W's property, which schedules are annexed hereto and made part hereof.
2. All property defined as Separate Property under the Domestic Relations Law of the State of New York, Section 236 (B) (1) (d), including property acquired prior to the marriage or by bequest, devise, descent, or gifts from third parties or interspousal gifts.
3. Compensation (damages) for personal injury, regardless of when and how suffered, including for pain and suffering, disability, disfigurement, lost wages and earning capacity, and punitive damages.
4. Property acquired after a Termination Event as defined in Article V herein.

5. All property purchased with or exchanged for Separate Property shall remain Separate Property.

6. The appreciation in value, income, and profits derived from Separate Property, whether by way of sale, exchange, investment, reinvestment, or otherwise, shall be and remain Separate Property regardless of the "active" or "passive" nature of said Separate Property and regardless of any direct or indirect contribution or effort of the other Party to the maintenance or appreciation of said Separate Property. Joint use of Separate Property or use of Marital Property to maintain Separate Property shall not give rise to joint ownership of such Separate Property or convert it to Marital Property unless such property is placed in joint names or the Parties agree in a writing executed with the same formality as this Agreement. Separate Property used to acquire jointly owned property will be returned and credited to the Party or Parties that contributed to the purchase of the jointly owned property, upon a sale of said property or upon the occurrence of a Termination Event as defined below.

6.1. With respect to premises _____, which apartment is A's separate property, the Parties agree that if apartment ___ is sold and a new apartment is purchased and title is taken in A's name alone or with W jointly or with any other person or person ("New Home"), New Home, together with improvements, shall be A's Separate Property. Thereafter, if New Home is sold and the Parties purchase a subsequent home (apartment or house) and use the proceeds of the sale of New Home to purchase any other future residence(s) in which title is taken in joint names or as tenants by the entirety, upon a "Termination Event," A shall be entitled to the return of the proceeds of sale of New Home, minus any monetary contributions from W. The difference between the proceeds of sale of the subsequently acquired apartment or home and of New Home, if any, shall be shared fifty percent (50%) to W and fifty percent (50%) to A.

6.2 The Parties acknowledge and agree that A owns fifty-one percent (51%) of his business which is known as _____ LLC ("_____"). _____ is located at _____. A's ownership interest in _____ is his separate property, and W acknowledges it as such Separate Property. In the event that A acquires additional stock in _____ during the course of the marriage and prior to a Termination Event by purchase, gift, or inheritance or if A purchases said stock with funds belonging to _____, his interest in _____ or personal funds he acquired before or during the marriage, A's increased ownership of _____ shall be and remain A's Separate Property.

7.   Any and all retirement accounts, including but not limited to, pensions, 401(k), and IRA accounts, only to the extent of the value in such accounts obtained before the marriage (the "Premarriage Value") and the subsequent appreciation in value, if any, on such Premarriage Value due to passive market forces.

8.   If the Parties comingle any of their Separate Property, such Separate Property shall not become Marital Property unless the Parties agree in writing that it becomes Marital Property or they place the comingled property in joint names or in a joint account.

9.   The Parties agree that under no circumstances shall their Separate Property be considered Marital Property or community property or quasicommunity property or otherwise be subject to any claim or right of the other in the event of a Termination Event herein but shall remain the Parties' Separate Property, notwithstanding any contrary provision of the law of any jurisdiction. Each of them shall own, hold, and freely dispose of their Separate Property, wher-

ever it may be situated and whether it is now owned by him or her or may hereafter be acquired by him or her, free from all rights of the other therein under the laws of any jurisdiction. Each of them hereby waives, renounces, and releases any and all rights which he or she may have under the laws of any jurisdiction in and to the other's Separate Property in the event of a Termination Event, including, without limitation, rights to Marital Property, equitable distribution, a distributive share, community property, quasicommunity property, or any other rights, whether they be vested, contingent, or inchoate.

ARTICLE IV—MARITAL PROPERTY

A.   The following shall constitute the Parties' Marital Property:

1.   All property acquired during the marriage until the occurrence of a Termination Event that is not Separate Property as set forth in Article III above.

2.   Except as provided for in Article III above, all property acquired by the Parties after the marriage and prior to the occurrence of a Termination Event whether said property is real, personal, or mixed and wherever situated.

3.   Except as otherwise provided herein, the voluntary contribution of Separate Property to acquire property in joint names with right of survivorship or as tenants by the entirety.

4.   All property designated by the Parties as Marital Property in a written agreement, executed and acknowledged by the Parties with the same formality as required to conform with Section 236 (B) (3) of the New York State Domestic Relations Law.

ARTICLE V—TERMINATION EVENT

A. Termination Event under this Agreement is defined to be the soonest occurrence of the following events:

1. The date on which a Party provides the other Party with written notice that he or she intends to dissolve the marriage. Said notice shall be delivered by United States Postal Service by registered or certified mail, return, receipt requested, or overnight courier with proof of delivery thereon.
2. The commencement of an action for divorce, separation, or annulment.
3. The execution of a written separation agreement, executed in compliance with Section 236 (B) (3) of the New York State Domestic Relations Law.

ARTICLE VI—RIGHT OF THE PARTIES UPON THE OCCURRENCE OF A TERMINATION EVENT

A. In the event of a Termination Event:

1. The marital home shall be placed on the market for sale within one year from the date of the Termination Event, and the net proceeds of the sale shall be distributed in accordance with the terms of this Agreement. W has the right to remain in the marital residence up to one (1) year following a Termination Event.
2. Each Party shall retain his or her Separate Property, and the other Party agrees not to make any claim in or to such property. Each of the Parties hereby waives, releases, and renounces (notwithstanding any contrary provision of the law of any jurisdiction) any right to or interest in the other Party's Separate Property, including, without limitation, an equitable distribution, a distributive share, or any other portion thereof or interest therein, whether as Marital

Property, community property, quasicommunity property, or otherwise.

3. W shall be entitled to maintenance in accordance with Section 236 (B) (3) of the New York State Domestic Relations Law.

4. Except as otherwise provided in this Agreement, all Martial Property as defined in Article IV of this Agreement shall be divided between the Parties in accordance with the Domestic Relations Law of the State of New York in accordance with Sec. 236 (B) as it is presently constituted. The date of the occurrence of a Termination Event shall, for all purposes, constitute the valuation date.

5. If within thirty (30) days following a Termination Event, the Parties cannot agree on the value or how to effectuate the distribution of any or all their Marital Property, then each asset in dispute will be sold at arm's length to a third party and the net proceeds of the sale divided equally between the Parties. If the Parties cannot agree on the sale price of the property and/or the method of sale, then within sixty (60) days of a Termination Event, each Party shall choose a qualified broker or appraiser. Each broker or appraiser shall seek to reach agreement with the other as to the price and method of sale. If the two brokers or appraisers fail to agree within twenty (20) days of their appointment, the two brokers or appraisers shall choose a third broker or appraiser who shall sell the property for maximum price reasonably obtainable given the market conditions at the time of sale. The third broker's value or price will govern.

6. In the event that either Party shall die following the occurrence of a Termination Event but prior to entry of a decree of dissolution of the marriage, Marital Property shall be divided between the surviving spouse and the deceased spouse's estate as set forth in this Agreement as if a decree of dissolution had been entered on the date of death of the deceased spouse.

ARTICLE VII—DISCLOSURE OF ASSETS

Each Party confirms that he or she has received sufficient financial disclosure of the other Party's assets from the other Party and such other Party's attorneys that the other Party offered to respond fully and directly to all questions such Party and such Party's attorneys might have concerning such financial information, that such Party regards such information and the information set forth on Schedules A and B attached hereto, as sufficient disclosure, both in form and substance, and that, upon the advice of such Party's independent counsel, such Party is fully aware of and understands all the rights which he or she is surrendering or releasing pursuant to this Agreement. Each Party agrees that to the extent that any assets, income, or liabilities have not been disclosed for any reason to either of them, knowledge of such additional assets or liabilities would not be relevant in their determination to enter into this Agreement and to be married and shall be no bar to the enforcement of this Agreement or any provision hereof because their knowledge of the assets and liabilities which have been disclosed is sufficient basis for this Agreement.

ARTICLE VIII—GOVERNING LAW

The Parties hereto agree that all questions arising under or with respect to this Agreement and its interpretation or enforceability shall be governed by the substantive laws of the State of New York (without considering or applying the conflicts of law principles of any state). The Parties agree that New York law shall govern the interpretation and enforceability of this Agreement regardless of where the Parties shall live from time to time during the marriage or at the time of its dissolution.

ARTICLE IX—VOLUNTARY EXECUTION

Each Party acknowledges that this Agreement is fair and equitable, that it is being entered into voluntarily, and that it is not the result of any duress or undue influence. Each Party has read this Agreement prior to its execution, understands it, and is fully aware of the rights that he or she is or may be releasing pursuant to the terms of this Agreement.

ARTICLE X—ENTIRE UNDERSTANDING OF THE PARTIES

A. This Agreement sets forth the entire understanding of the Parties and supersedes all other agreements, written or oral, between the Parties, including, without limitation, any implied or other agreements arising in connection with any period of cohabitation. The Parties affirm that no agreements have been entered into between them prior to the date of this Agreement. Neither Party has relied upon any representation of the other Party except such as are specifically mentioned in this Agreement.

B. Each of the Parties acknowledges and confirms that both Parties actively participated equally in the negotiation of this Agreement, and should any ambiguities exist in this Agreement, the same shall not be constructed against the Party whose attorneys prepared the initial draft of this Agreement.

C. Neither Party shall make any application in or to any court or tribunal inconsistent with the provisions thereof, and in the event of a separation or divorce of the Parties or other dissolution of the Parties' marriage, the provisions hereof shall be incorporated but not merged in such divorce decree.

ARTICLE XI—AMENDMENT OR REVOCATION

This Agreement may not be amended or revoked except by an instrument in writing signed by both of the Parties and acknowledged and witnessed with the same formalities of this Agreement, expressly modifying or revoking one or more or all the provisions of this Agreement.

ARTICLE XII—BINDING EFFECT

All the provisions of this Agreement shall inure to the benefit of and be binding upon the Parties and their respective heirs, issue, next of kin, distributes, executors, administrators, legal and personal representatives, successors, and assigns.

ARTICLE XIII—PARTIAL INVALIDITY

In the event that any term, provision, clause, subparagraph, paragraph, subdivision, or section of this Agreement is declared illegal, void, or unenforceable, it shall not affect or impair the other terms, provisions, clauses, subparagraphs, paragraphs, subdivisions, or sections of this Agreement. The doctrine of severability shall be applied. The Parties do not intend, by this statement, to imply the illegality, voidness, or unenforceability of any term, provision, clause, subparagraph, paragraph, subdivision, or section of this Agreement.

ARTICLE XIV—FURTHER DOCUMENTS

Each of the Parties, without cost to the other, shall at any time, and from time to time, hereafter execute and deliver any and all further instruments and assurances and perform any act that the other Party may reasonably request for the purpose of giving full force and effect to the provision of this Agreement.

ARTICLE XV—LEGAL FEES AND INDEPENDENT COUNSEL

1. W declares that she has been represented by independent counsel in the negotiation and execution of this Agreement, having been represented by _____, and that she fully understands her legal rights and liabilities.
2. A declares that he has been represented by _____ and that he fully understands his legal rights and obligations. Each Party represents that

he has carefully read this Agreement and understands its provisions.

3. A agrees that he shall be responsible for W's legal fees incurred in connection with the negotiation, preparation, and execution of this Agreement.

4. If either Party contests the validity of this Agreement or any provision thereof, that Party shall be responsible for the reasonable value of any legal services rendered on behalf of either Party by reason of the other Parties successfully contesting the validity of this Agreement or any provision hereof, whether such services arise out of court action or otherwise, and shall be paid by the Party unsuccessfully contesting the validity of this Agreement or any provision hereof.

IN WITNESS THEREOF, the Parties have hereunto set their respective hands and seals as of the day and year first above written.

W	A
Witness as to	Witness as to
W:	A:

STATE OF NEW YORK
SS:
COUNTY OF NEW YORK

On this _____, before me, the undersigned, a Notary Public for said State, personally appeared W, personally known to be or proved to me on the basis of satisfactory evidence to be the individual whose name is subscribed to the within instrument and acknowledged to me that she executed the same in her capacity and that her signature on the instrument, the individual, or person upon behalf of which the individual acted executed the instrument.

Notary Public

STATE OF NEW YORK
ss:
COUNTY OF NEW YORK

On this _____, before me, the undersigned, a Notary Public for said State, personally appeared A, personally known to be or proved to me on the basis of satisfactory evidence to be the individual whose name is subscribed to the within instrument and acknowledged to me that he executed the same in his capacity and that his signature on the instrument, the individual, or person upon behalf of which the individual acted executed the instrument.

Notary Public

SCHEDULE A
Assets
Liabilities

SCHEDULE B
Assets
Liabilities

Islamic Marriage Contract

Here is a sample of what a marriage contract can contain:

In the name of Allah, the Beneficent, the Merciful Allah (SWT) says, "And of His signs is that He created for you mates from your own selves that you take comfort in them, and He ordained affection and mercy between you."

In the Holy Quran 30: 21, Prophet Muhammad (PBUH) said, "He who marries attains half of his religion, and he should fear Allah in the second half [of his religion]." By the book of Allah (SWT) the Almighty and the tradition of His prophet, Muhammad (peace be upon him and his holy household), this marriage contract was established on the _____ day of _____ in the year _____ CE corresponding to the _____ day of _____ in the year _____ AH in the city of _____, the state of _____, and the county of _____, between the groom and bride outlined below and under the conditions that have been agreed upon within this document, in accordance with Islamic law based on the school of thought of Ahl al-Bayt (peace be upon them).

Groom's information and signature   Bride's information and signature
First Name: First Name:
Surname: Surname:
Date of Birth: Date of Birth:
Place of Birth: Place of Birth:
Dowry Advanced Portion: _____
Deferred Portion: _____
Due at the nearest of the two terms (divorce or death) upon the ability to do so upon request of the marriage contract.

This contract has been agreed upon by the Council of Shia Muslim Scholars of North America at the tenth annual conference.

Agreed-Upon Conditions

As a result of the numerous experiences and studies in this field from experts who are engaged in such services, the attendees of the tenth annual conference of the Council of Shia Muslim Scholars in North America, who participated in the final resolution, endorsed these terms and conditions in hopes that following them will be an important factor in achieving marital happiness and steering the marriage away from harm with the will of the Almighty.

The terms and conditions are not limited to those mentioned herein; they are suggestions given by the experts, and they are not binding unless agreed upon by both parties. The only terms considered binding are those agreed upon by both parties that are within this document or have been added hereto.

It is highly recommended for both parties, seeking marriage within this contract, to learn and to have a full picture of the rights, obligations, and manners of marriage in Islam. It is also requested that both parties review the civil law of their state so that they may understand their rights and obligations from a legal standpoint.

Based upon this:

❖ The husband grants the wife, within this marriage contract, transferrable, irrevocable agency in divorcing herself Islamic divorce with supervision and endorsement by a qualified religious scholar in the matter of Islamic laws.

❖ The agency given in this agreement is limited to the implementation of any conditions mentioned below.

List of Conditions

Bride's signature   Groom's signature

1. If the husband refuses to provide the basic necessities of life for the wife for a period of _____ months, regardless of the reasons. This could be if he cannot be forced to pay or if he is not willing to commit to doing it voluntarily. _____ _____
2. If the husband refuses his wife her conjugal rights for a period of _____ months without a religiously acceptable excuse. _____ _____
3. Due to direct or indirect abuse by the husband to a point the wife cannot continue in the marriage. _____ _____
4. If the husband is afflicted with an illness, which may cause risk to the wife. _____ _____
5. If the husband loses his mental capacity (becomes insane) in cases where there is no automatic right of annulment. _____ _____
6. If the husband becomes sterile or it is obvious during the marriage that he is, which would render it impossible to produce children. This rule will apply only if there are no children already born to the couple. _____ _____
7. If the husband is imprisoned for a period that is considered unbearable for the wife. _____ _____
8. The husband's addiction to anything harmful, which renders the marriage hard to continue and unbearable for the wife. _____ _____
9. If the husband's whereabouts remain unknown for a period of one year and upon verification and notification. _____ _____
10. If the husband takes another wife without the consent of the present wife. _____ _____
11. If the husband prevents/hinders the wife from practicing her religious duties. _____ _____

12. In the case that the husband willingly divorces his wife according to civil law but abstains from divorcing her according to Islamic law. _____ _____

Additional Conditions

Bride's signature   Groom's signature

Notice(s):

_____
_____
_____
_____
_____
_____

Signatures   Full Name
Signature   Date

Husband _____
Wife _____
Wife's Guardian/Representative _____
Witness _____
Witness _____

GLOSSARY OF TERMS

abandonment/discard. The act of leaving a relationship or marriage without warning.

Allah. *Allah* is the standard Arabic word used for God and is used by Arabic-speaking Christians and Jews as well. It is the word used for the Creator of the heavens and the earth.

Alhamdullilah. All praise to Allah (God).

apostate. One who renounces their religion.

Asperger's syndrome. A developmental disorder related to autism and characterized with high intelligence but less-than-interactive social skills.

cluster B axis II (cluster B). Dramatic, overemotional, unpredictable thinking or behavior and includes borderline personality disorder and narcissistic personality disorder. Axis II includes compulsive and obsessive behaviors and paranoia.

covert narcissist. Someone who has an overexaggerated view of their own importance, devalues others, but behaves in a way that hides this undesirable quality to gain trust.

desertion. The act of removing financial support when leaving a marriage or relationship.

endemic. A disease that is ongoing and one can expect its occurrence in the population.

epidemic. A disease that is sudden, widespread, and unpredictable.

Hadith. Accounts of conversations and/or actions and behaviors of Prophet Muhammad.

gaslighting. An attempt to rewrite the facts or change someone's view of what actually occurred.

halal. Religiously permissible.

Imam. The leader in the Muslim community; he will often lead prayers, but others can lead prayers as well.

iman. A believer's faith.

Istakara **prayer.** Prayer to seek counsel before making a decision.

love-bombing. Showering someone with affection, gifts, compliments in order to manipulate them or those around them.

malignant narcissist. Someone who has an overexaggerated view of their own importance, devalues others, but is extreme to the point of mental and/or physical abuse.

masjid/mosque. Place of worship for Muslims.

Muslim. One who submits to the will of Allah/God.

narcissist. A person who has an overexaggerated view of their own importance and is hyperfocused on receiving attention, adoration, or accolades while devaluing others.

narcissistic personality disorder (NPD). One of several types of diagnosis of antisocial behavior that is a mental condition of an inflation of one's sense of importance, excessive attention-seeking, troublesome relationships, and devaluing others.

nikah. The marriage ceremony to sign the marriage contract.

PBUH. Peace and blessings be upon Him.

pillars of Islam (5). Shahada (declaration of faith), salat (prayer), zakat (charity), sawm (fasting), and hajj (pilgrimage).

psychopath. Extreme lack of empathy, along with manipulative, charming, and exploitative behavior.

PTSD. Post-traumatic stress disorder is the lasting effects such is dreams, stress, depression, or anxiety from an event that caused mental, physical, or emotional distress, injury, or trauma.

Quran. The religious book followed by Muslims believed to be the Word of Allah as dictated to Prophet Muhammad by the angel Gabriel.

Satan. This is also the name of Iblis, the devil, who performs demonic acts to lure believers away from Allah/God.

salat. The formal way of prayer for Muslims. The obligation is to pray five times per day.

sociopath. Unofficial term to describe a person with antisocial personality disorder.

spirit-breaking/demeaning. To destroy someone's confidence, sense of independence, and self-esteem.

Sunnah. The life and teachings of Prophet Muhammad. The way of life practiced by Suni Muslims is guided by the Sunnah.

taqwa. Being conscious of God, God-fearing.

wali/wakil. A person who works as an adviser to a woman who is seeking marriage. He may be a male relative or a leader in the community.

ABOUT THE AUTHOR

Although Kaleema spent 27 years writing grants and health care policy, it wasn't until she experienced a planned abandonment on a family vacation—that she was compelled to write her first book. This book was written in real time and became an organic step to healing from the trauma of abandonment. The women she interviewed became her sisters in the struggle to survive as they all navigated from tragedy to triumph. Kaleema's own journey included lodging a public complaint that resulted in an invitation to write a seven-series column. Kaleema took great care to honor the men who protect women from psychological, economic, and spiritual abuse. She has a passion for volunteerism and cohosts an interfaith radio show that promotes community involvement. Kaleema is available for speaking engagements.